THE OLD VIC THEATRE COLLECTION
VOLUME THREE

TOO CLEVER BY HALF

or

THE DIARY OF A SCOUNDREL

•

By Alexander Ostrovsky

•

English Version by Rodney Ackland

•

Afterword by Daniel Gerould

THEATRE BOOK PUBLISHERS
211 West 71 Street, New York, NY 10023

Library of Congress Cataloging-in-Publication Data
Ostrovsky, Aleksandr Nikolaevich, 1823-1886.
    Too clever by half, or The diary of a scoundrel.
    (The Old Vic Theatre collection; v. 3)
    Translation of: Na vsiakogao mudretsa dovol'no prostoty.
    Previously published as: Enough stupidity in every wise
man; Even a wise man stumbles; Even the wise can err.
    I. Title. II. Title: Diary of a scoundrel. III. Series.
PG337.08N2513 1988   891.72'3   88-6254
ISBN 1-55783-023-1

APPLAUSE THEATRE BOOK PUBLISHERS
211 West 71st Street
New York, NY 10023

122 Kennington Rd.
London, England SE11

CONTENTS

• • •

THE OLD VIC THEATRE COLLECTION
published by Applause Theatre Books

Available at all fine booksellers.
Orders may also be placed by post direct from the Old Vic
or from Applause Theatre Books.

TOO
CLEVER
BY
HALF

TOO CLEVER BY HALF
By Alexander Ostrovsky

Yegor Dimitrich Gloumov	Alex Jennings
	Aden Gillett
	(last two weeks)
Glafira Klimovna Gloumova	Janet Henfrey
Styopka	Charles Lewsen
Neel Fedoseitch Mamaev	John Stratton
Kleopatra Ilvovna Mamaev	Linda Marlowe
Kroutitsky	Timothy Barlow
Ivan Ivanovitch Gorodoulin	Peter Guinness
Sofia Ignatievna Tourousina	Rosalind Knight
Mashenka	Julia Bardsley
Yegor Vassilitch Kourchaev	Aden Gillett
Golutvin	Phelim McDermott
Maniefa	Celia Gore Booth
Matriosha	Katharine Page
Lubinka	Ann Way
Grigori	Charles Lewsen
Director	Richard Jones
Designer	Richard Hudson

Characters

YEGOR DIMITRICH GLOUMOV,
a young man

GLAFIRA KLIMOVNA GLOUMOVA,
his mother

STYOPKA,
their servant

NEEL FEDOSEITCH MAMAEV,
a wealthy gentleman, a distant relative of Gloumov

KLEOPATRA ILVOVNA MAMEVA,
his wife

KROUTITZKY,
an old man of importance

IVAN IVANOVITCH GORODOULIN,
a young man of importance

SOFIA IGNATIEVNA TOUROUSINA,
a wealthy widow, the daughter of a merchant

MASHENKA,
her niece

YEGOR VASSILITCH KOURCHAEV,
a Hussar

GOLUTVIN,
a man without an occupation

MANIEFA,
a seeress

Companions to Madame Tourousina:
MATRIOSHA
LUBINKA

MAMAEV'S MANSERVANT
GRIGORI,
Madame Tourousina's manservant

THE TIME: *the 1860's*
THE PLACE: *Moscow and outside Moscow.*

A C T O N E, *Scene 1: The Gloumov apartment.*
Scene 2: The Mamaevs' house.

A C T T W O, *Scene 1: Madame Tourousina's house, outside*
Moscow. Scene 2: The Gloumov apartment.

A C T T H R E E, *Madame Tourousina's house.*

ACT ONE

SCENE 1

The living-room of the GLOUMOV *apartment in Moscow. It is rather poorly furnished except for one or two articles which would be more in place in a fashionable drawing-room. There are two doors, one on right, opening on to the hall, the second into the other rooms of the apartment.* STYOPKA, *the servant, lolls in his shirt sleeves, picking his teeth.* GLOUMOV *is pacing the room. Going to the door up-stage, he calls out:*

GLOUMOV. Get on with those letters, Mamma!

MADAME G., *off.* There's not a bite to eat in the house!

GLOUMOV. We'll have plenty to eat if you do what I tell you.

MADAME G., *entering.* I wish you'd find someone else to write them.

GLOUMOV. Oh, don't argue!

MADAME G. *to* STYOPKA. Get up! Lolling about in here! Your place is in the kitchen. The samovar's not been polished for weeks.

STYOPKA. No, and I've not been paid for weeks. Not since the old man died.

MADAME G. Don't speak of your sainted master like that! God rest his soul. Go on, go away, I hate the sight of you.
Going to the desk she gets out paper, pen and ink.

STYOPKA. Well, I don't like it here. I'm not used to living in pokey apartments. I'm the only one that stayed on with you when you moved to this place. You ought to be grateful to me.

1

MADAME G. The greatest calamity that ever happened to this country was the freeing of the serfs!

STYOPKA. I wouldn't stay at all if it wasn't for the young master. It's only a matter of time before he'll put us on our feet in a fine mansion again.

GLOUMOV. Well, go and arrange that business with Mr. Mamaev's manservant. How much of your savings have you got left?

STYOPKA. Only about 200 roubles, sir.

GLOUMOV. Nonsense. You've got at least 500. Lend me another fifty.

STYOPKA, *grumbling under his breath, produces an old purse and fumbles in it.*

MADAME G., *who has been copying out a letter.* What's this word, Yegor? I can't understand your writing. Kourchaev is a *what?*

GLOUMOV, *looking over her shoulder.* "Vile seducer."

Taking the money from STYOPKA.

Thanks. . . . Here you are, here's five for the Mamaev job, five to replenish the larder, and two for yourself.

STYOPKA. Thank you very much, sir.

He goes towards the door upstage.

GLOUMOV. And don't pay for the food unless you have to.

STYOPKA, *off.* Very good, sir.

MADAME G., *looking after him.* Disgusting dolt!

To GLOUMOV.

Give me ten of those roubles. I haven't had a new hat since your father died, and then I only had one every three months. Stingy old devil!

GLOUMOV *gives her the money. She grabs it from him.*

GLOUMOV. Get on with the letters, do!

MADAME G. What's the good? Madame Tourousina will never let you marry her niece. The dowry of 20,000 roubles—

GLOUMOV. That's exactly why I've chosen her.

MADAME G. They could get a prince or at least a general for that. Kourchaev won't get her either, so I can't see the point of these anonymous letters about him. Your own second cousin, too!

GLOUMOV. As if that mattered to you! You know his type—a typical Hussar—if he had money he'd only lose it at cards.

MADAME G. If I could see any *good* coming of them.

GLOUMOV. That's my business.

MADAME G. What chance do you think there is?

GLOUMOV. Every sort of chance. My dear Mamma, you know me: I'm intelligent and malicious, envious of anyone better off than myself. In fact, I take after you. Yet what did I do when Papa was alive and we had money? Nothing but hang about feeling bored and bad-tempered and writing lampoons on everybody in Moscow. Now that I've got to make a place for myself I've realised it's not enough to make fun of all the stupid people who run this city. One must know how to take advantage of their idiocies. Unfortunately it's no good thinking of a career in Moscow. The only thing they do here is talk. All one can hope for is a bride with a fat dowry and an important job with no work and a fat salary.

MADAME G. Where are you going to get that?

GLOUMOV. In the Civil Service, of course. But how do people succeed in Moscow? Not by doing anything, merely by talking. Talk is the only thing that matters here. And nobody likes talking better than I do. So what is to prevent my success in the hot air spouters' Paradise? Nothing.

MADAME G. Well, stop talking and let me write these anonymous letters.

GLOUMOV, *moving about the room looking for something.* Have you moved my diary, Mamma?

MADAME G. It's on the table over there.

GLOUMOV, *taking it.* Thank you. What a mistake I made with my lampoons and malicious epigrams! I've finished with all that!
Throwing himself into a chair.

From now on it's to be nauseating, toadying flattery, the only language the élite of Moscow understand. I shall begin with Madame Tourousina's circle. When I've squeezed that dry, I shall move on to the next.

MADAME G. Oh stop, my head's aching. What's this? Kourchaev's a what? "Well-known"
trying to decipher it.
"*criminal?*"

GLOUMOV. No, liberal, liberal. . . . But do you know what I intend to do, Mamma, while I'm flattering these stupid fools? I must have some outlet for my feelings or I should go mad.
Holding up the book.
It will be this, my diary. All the bitterness that boils up in my soul I shall get rid of here, and there'll be nothing but honey on my lips. Alone, in the silence of the night, I shall write these chronicles of human triviality entirely for myself. I shall be both author and reader.
There is a loud peal at the front door bell.

MADAME G. Styopka!
STYOPKA *lounges in, pulling on his jacket.*

STYOPKA: It's that military gentleman in the Hussars. I saw him getting out of a cab with another gentleman. They both looked tipsy to me.

MADAME G., *to* GLOUMOV. Kourchaev! What does he want?

GLOUMOV. Nothing, I dare say. To show off his stupidity.

MADAME G., *following* STYOPKA. Do up your coat, take those sunflower seeds out of your mouth! Ten years ago you'd have got a good beating!

STYOPKA, *going into the hall.* Well, it's not ten years ago.

MADAME G., *hurrying back to the table.* I'd better hide those letters! And Yegor, put that diary away. You don't want people prying into it.

GLOUMOV. Leave them, leave them, Mamma.

STYOPKA, *announcing.* Mr. Kourchaev and Mr. Golutvin.
KOURCHAEV *is a typical Hussar of the period. Tall, slim,*

with a military bearing and vacuous expression. He is in that pleasant stage of intoxication which shows itself in an unwonted enthusiasm and expansiveness. His friend, a few years older, dressed in an exaggeration of the latest fashion which borders on the ludicrous, has had an equal amount to drink.

KOURCHAEV. Gloumov, my dear fellow, I want you to meet a very great friend of mine—oh, a thousand pardons, Madame Gloumova.

Clicking his heels and kissing her hand.

Are you keeping in the best of health?

MADAME G. Not too well. . . . It's only six weeks since my sainted husband was taken from me, God rest his soul. But I'm bearing up somehow for the sake of Yegor, poor boy I'm bearing up. . . .

KOURCHAEV. Allow me to present a very great friend of mine—Golutvin.

GOLUTVIN, *kissing* MADAME GLOUMOVA's *hand*. Enchantée, Madame.

GLOUMOV, *to* STYOPKA, *idly watching in the doorway*. Styopka, go and attend to that job. At once, do you hear me?

STYOPKA. Very good, sir.

Goes out.

KOURCHAEV, *leading* GOLUTVIN *towards* GLOUMOV. I know you'll like each other. Golutvin's a devilish clever fellow. Gloumov —Golutvin.

Almost pushing GOLUTVIN *into* GLOUMOV's *arms*.

There, I'm entrusting him to you.

GLOUMOV, *turning and putting his diary into a drawer*. I can't accept the responsibility.

He adds.

This isn't the first time I've met Mr. Golutvin.

GOLUTVIN. I don't think I cared for the tone of voice.

MADAME G., *sotto voce*. The poor boy's not himself since he lost his sainted father, God rest his soul. Pray be seated both of you. If you'll excuse me, I have some correspondence to finish.

She seats herself at the desk and continues writing during the following scene, occasionally glancing up at KOURCHAEV.

GOLUTVIN. ⎱ Merci, merci, Madame. Trop gentille, trop aimable.

KOURCHAEV. ⎰ Certainly, certainly.... Sit here, Golutvin.

GLOUMOV. May I ask to what I'm indebted for this visit? I have very little time to spare, gentlemen. What's it about?
He sits down.

GOLUTVIN, *after exchanging glances with* KOURCHAEV. Mon cher ami, have you any verses?

GLOUMOV. Verses? You must have come to the wrong place.

GOLUTVIN. Mais non, mais non! Vous êtes trop modeste, mon cher.

GLOUMOV, *to* KOURCHAEV, *who, seated at the table, has picked up a pencil and is drawing something.* I say, do you mind not scribbling on my papers?

KOURCHAEV. My dear Yegor, apologies. . . . Now look here, we know perfectly well you've got some of those—what are they called? Um, you know, funny verses about fellows.

GOLUTVIN. Lampoons.
Turning to GLOUMOV.
In a word, my dear sir, we want lampoons—you've got them.

GLOUMOV. I'm sorry. I've none at all.

KOURCHAEV. Now, now, come on, we know. . . . Several fellows have told us. You've got a lot of devilish funny lampoons on everybody in town. Be a good fellow and help my very dear friend, Golutvin here. He wants to get a job writing the gossip column in a newspaper.

GLOUMOV. Oh, does he?
To GOLUTVIN.
Have you ever written anything?

GOLUTVIN. *Anything?* I've written everything. Novels, stories, plays, articles, epics——

GLOUMOV. Have you had them published?

GOLUTVIN. Oh no, they've none of them been published.

KOURCHAEV. They're much too good, that's the trouble.

GLOUMOV. Have you read them?

KOURCHAEV. No, but he's told me about them——

GOLUTVIN, *to* GLOUMOV, *interrupting*. Nobody's interested in anything but scandal today. So I want to start on that now. Writing scandalous paragraphs.

GLOUMOV. Oh, I shouldn't do that. It might be dangerous.

GOLUTVIN. Dangerous? What do you mean—that I might be set upon at night, attacked on my way home?

GLOUMOV. You'd undoubtedly get a few horsewhippings.

GOLUTVIN, *after a slight pause*. Never in Moscow, my dear friend, we leave that sort of thing to other—less civilised cities.

GLOUMOV. Well, go on then, write.

GOLUTVIN. But whom am I to write about? I don't know anybody.

KOURCHAEV. Look here, Yegor, we've heard that you've got some sort of diary in which you've pulled everybody to pieces——

GOLUTVIN. I hear it's the most delicious, malicious gossip in Moscow. *Do—do* lend it to me.

GLOUMOV. I haven't a diary.

KOURCHAEV. Now come on, you can't keep up this pretence with us.

GOLUTVIN. All I want is the material. Think of the money we could make with your material and my talent.

KOURCHAEV. Be a good fellow, Yegor. He really needs the money. He has to drink at other fellows' expense. It's humiliating for him.

GOLUTVIN. And I want to work—to work! All I need is the material.

GLOUMOV, *getting up.* I have none.

Taking up a paper from in front of KOURCHAEV.

What's this picture of a hippopotamus?

KOURCHAEV. It's not a hippopotamus. It's my respected uncle, Neel Fedoseitch Mamaev. Drawn as a hippopotamus, of course.

GOLUTVIN. Tell me, is he an interesting personality? Would he be of interest to me, for instance?

KOURCHAEV. He's a horrible old bore. He thinks himself the brainiest man in Moscow and all he does is lecture people for their own good.

GOLUTVIN. Is he rich? Important?

KOURCHAEV. That's the trouble, he's got a lot of money to leave so I'm always having to ask him for advice. Nothing gives him greater pleasure.

GOLUTVIN, *taking the drawing from* GLOUMOV. Excusez moi, monsieur. Now all we need is an amusing title for this picture and we'll sell it to the papers. Write underneath, er, now let me think of something really witty. . . . Write . . .

A flash of inspiration.

The Talking Hippopotamus.

KOURCHAEV *does so, laughing.* Talking hippopotamus. . . . But look here, we can't have it published. After all, he is my uncle.

GLOUMOV, *taking the paper from him, he slips it into his pocket.* And my cousin, incidentally.

GOLUTVIN. Tell me more about him. Has he other characteristics that I could satirise?

KOURCHAEV. In my opinion he's not all there. For three years he's been looking for a new apartment. He doesn't really want one. It's simply an excuse to go about talking and boring people—but it looks as if he's doing something, at least. He drives off in the morning, looks over about ten apartments, has a talk with the landlords and the porters, then he makes a round of the grocers' shops to taste the caviar and smoked herrings. He plants himself down and starts to bore the unfortunate shop assistants. The poor fellows don't know how to get him out of the shop, but he's delighted with himself and thinks he's spent a profitable morning.

Turning to GLOUMOV.

By the way, his wife, my Aunt Kleopatra, is in love with you.

GLOUMOV. Oh, really?

KOURCHAEV. She saw you at the opera the other day. "Who's that? she kept asking me. Her eyes were nearly popping out of her head and she practically twisted her neck off. . . . I mean it. . . . This is no joke, you know.

GLOUMOV. I'm not joking. It's you who treat everything as a joke.

KOURCHAEV. Well, anyway, you take my advice.

With a glance at MADAME GLOUMOVA, *then sotto voce.*

I should follow that up if I were you. . . . Now, are you going to let us see that diary of yours?

GLOUMOV. No.

KOURCHAEV. Be a good fellow.

GOLUTVIN. Just a tiny peep.

GLOUMOV *doesn't answer.*

Some lampoons then. . . .

Diminuendo.

Just one lampoon . . . an epigram.

GLOUMOV. I've told you I have none.

GOLUTVIN, *suddenly springing up and making for the door.*
Oh, what's the use of talking to him? Let's go and get some dinner.

Bowing to MADAME GLOUMOVA *on his way out.*

Bonjour, madame. Merci.

MADAME G., *smiling politely.* Going so soon?

Turning to KOURCHAEV.

Oh, this correspondence! My poor brain! Even my spelling goes. How many l's are there in "villainous"?

KOURCHAEV. Villainous—er—let me see . . . two.

MADAME G. Of course. Thank you.

KOURCHAEV. Can I be of assistance? Shall I have the letters
delivered for you?

MADAME G. You're too kind. I couldn't put you to so much
trouble. Good-bye. Come and see us again soon. Always
delighted to see you.
She holds out her hand which he kisses.

KOURCHAEV. Indeed I will.
He clicks his heels, and is on his way out when GLOUMOV
stops him.

GLOUMOV. What on earth are you doing with a creature like
that?

KOURCHAEV. Devilish clever fellow. I like clever people.

GLOUMOV. You've most certainly found one there.

KOURCHAEV. Clever enough for us anyway. Really intelligent
fellows wouldn't bother with fellows like us.
He goes.
GOLUTVIN *has been waiting for him outside the front door.
As soon as the door is closed* GLOUMOV *drops his stiff attitude, bursts into laughter and strides about the room in a
high state of elation.*

GLOUMOV. It's working, it's all working, Mamma! Exactly as
I'd planned. I knew Cousin Kleopatra had seen me from
her box. I took good care that she should. She got an excellent view of my profile and I tried to look exceedingly
romantic.

MADAME G. This Mamaev, her husband, he's the person you
must get hold of. Why should Kourchaev get a legacy from
him? *You* must get it instead, Yegor. Shall I send an anonymous letter to *him?*

GLOUMOV. No, no, I've got everything planned. I know all
about Mamaev. He has at least fifty nephews and cousins,
including myself whom he hasn't met yet. He picks on
one of them, makes a will in his favor until he gets sick
of him, then he forbids him the house, chooses another
one and renames his will again. . . . But Kourchaev won't
last long. This little drawing of a hippopotamus

taking it from his pocket
should prove very useful.
Replaces it carefully.
You see, once I'm friendly with the Mamaevs I'm on the
first rung of the ladder. Through them I can meet Kroutitzky
and Gorodoulin who are not only extremely important in
the Civil Service—*but*—they are intimate friends of Madame
Tourousina. And once I've gained entrance to her house,
there's nothing to stop me.

MADAME G. That's all very well, dear, but the most difficult
step is the first.

GLOUMOV. Don't worry, I've taken it. Mamaev's coming here
this morning.

MADAME G. What do you mean?

GLOUMOV. He likes looking over apartments. I found that out
some days ago. Styopka is out arranging with Mamaev's
servant to bring the old fellow here.
The front door bell rings.
Going towards the door.
If this is Madame Maniefa, be as nice to her as possible.
In fact, be more than nice to her.

MADAME G. Indeed I won't! Why should I lower myself in
front of a disgusting, common, creature? A low fortune-
teller reeking of vodka!

GLOUMOV. A "clairvoyante", Mamma. And a very useful ally.
She's going to tell fortunes at Madame Tourousina's next
Wednesday. Time enough for you to play the grand lady
when I'm married to Tourousina's niece. For the moment
all I ask is your help. You must treat Maniefa as if she
were an archbishop. When she moves about the room we
must support her under the armpits like acolytes when a
bishop's saying Mass. She expects that. And give her what's
left of the vodka.
He opens the door. An enormous woman with a florid com-
plexion, a magnificent shawl wrapped round her, is revealed
on the threshold. She is holding on to the doorpost and
breathing heavily.
Madame Maniefa! Mamma! It *is*! It's Madame Maniefa!

Our prayers are answered. Will you come in, Madame
Maniefa? Isn't this a great honour, Mamma?

MANIEFA, *coming ponderously into the room.* Are you fleeing
the vanities of the world, young man?

GLOUMOV. Oh, indeed I am. But I need your help, dear
Madame Maniefa—your holy influence. Mamma, get Madame Maniefa a chair.

MANIEFA, *lowering herself into it with painful groans and
grunts.* Oh, my back! Ah! . . . that's better.
Rubs her diaphragm and belches.
It's that tea they gave me where I called last. Something
told me that would be an evil house.
She takes no notice whatever of MADAME GLOUMOVA *who
has been madly bowing and curtseying.*

GLOUMOV. Do you think a little drop of vodka would put you
right? Mamma, bring the vodka for Madame Maniefa.
MADAME GLOUMOVA *goes to get it.*

GLOUMOV. You do too much, you know. You ought to think
of yourself more.

MANIEFA, *her eyes fixed on the bottle which* MADAME GLOU-
MOVA *has produced.* Flee—flee from the vanities of the
world. . . . At one pious household I was in today they
gave me money for charity. They gave alms through my
hands. The holy saints prefer alms to flow through holy
hands instead of sinful ones.
She watches intently as MADAME GLOUMOVA *pours her out
some vodka.*

GLOUMOV. And such holy hands! . . .
Taking out some money.
May I humbly offer twenty roubles?

MANIEFA, *putting the money in her bag.* Blessed are they that
give. . . . Could you make it thirty?

GLOUMOV. Twenty-five.
MANIEFA *without replying, holds out her hand for the other
five roubles and drains the vodka in one gulp.* STYOPKA
*comes in, his arms filled with provisions—loaves, cooked
sausages, smoked herrings, a bottle of wine.*

STYOPKA. It's all arranged, sir. The gentleman's on his way here now.

GLOUMOV. Madame Maniefa, will you stay and share our humble meal?

MANIEFA, *her eyes greedily on the food.* A few crusts—that's all I need.

GLOUMOV. Perhaps you'd like to rest first? . . . Mamma, take Madame Maniefa to your room.
Placing a hand under the Prophetess's armpit and signalling to his mother to do the same on the other side—which she does with a surreptitious grimace.

MANIEFA. Ooooh . . . my back. . . . God's chosen ones are sorely afflicted. . . .
They lead her to the door.
Flee . . . from the vanities of the world.
She glances over her shoulder at the vodka bottle.

GLOUMOV. Mamma! Take the vodka bottle with you! Madame Maniefa is worn out with her holy work.
MADAME GLOUMOVA gives her son a look of suppressed fury, darts back, and snatches up the bottle and glass. They lead MANIEFA off. STYOPKA lays out the food on a table. GLOUMOV comes back.
You didn't *pay* for that, Styopka?

STYOPKA. Bless you no, sir. It's from Smirnoff's where Mr. Kourchaev shops. I put it down to his account.

GLOUMOV, *tasting a piece of smoked herring.* Good. How much did you give Mr. Mamaev's servant?

STYOPKA. Three roubles.

GLOUMOV. I must put all this down.
Gets his diary and sits at the table with it.
Let's see, Maniefa—twenty-five roubles, Mamaev's servant —three roubles. . . .
The front door bell rings.

STYOPKA, *going to answer it.* That'll be him. . . .

MADAME G., *putting her head round the door.* Lying on my bed! I shall have to have it disinfected now.

GLOUMOV. Don't come in till I call you. Go back and stay with her.

MADAME G., *withdrawing.* Disgusting creature—I was saving that vodka for my birthday.

SERVANT, *appearing.* I've brought Mr. Mamaev—I don't know how he'll take it. I told him this was a *nice* apartment.

GLOUMOV. Here you are—here's another rouble.

SERVANT. Very good, sir.
Goes out.

GLOUMOV. Go on, Styopka—into the kitchen.

STYOPKA, *going.* Good luck, sir. . . .
Sotto voce.
He's a silly old fool. I've seen him.
GLOUMOV *sits at the desk and pretends to be working.* MAMAEV, *a short fat gentleman, overcome with the heat and the climb up the stairs, enters followed by his servant.*

MAMAEV, *mopping his brow.* What's this—a bachelor's apartment?

GLOUOV, *bowing to him and continuing with his work.* Yes, it is.

MAMAEV, *ignoring him.* Wouldn't be so bad, decently furnished, but what's the good of a bachelor apartment to me?
To servant.
What did you want to bring me here for?

GLOUMOV, *pushing forward a chair and again busying himself with his writing.* Do sit down.

MAMAEV, *sitting down without looking at him.* Thanks. . . .
What's the point of bringing me here?

SERVANT. Sorry, sir.

MAMAEV. You know perfectly well a bachelor apartment's no good to me. A place like this for a Minister of State! . . . You know quite well that Madame Mamaeva likes to keep open house.

SERVANT. Sorry, sir.

MAMAEV. Where's the drawing-room?

SERVANT. Sorry, sir.

MAMAEV. Don't "sorry sir" me! . . . Damn stupidity.
As though seeing GLOUMOV *for the first time.*
There you are, you see, there's a man sitting here writing.
We're probably disturbing him only he's too polite to say
so; and it's all your fault, you silly fool!

GLOUMOV. Please don't blame him! I happened to hear him
inquiring about an apartment in this building and I suggested mine. I'm afraid I didn't realise you were a family
man.

MAMAEV. Are you the owner of this apartment?

GLOUMOV. Yes.

MAMAEV. What do you want to let it for then?

GLOUMOV. It's beyond my means.

MAMAEV. Why take it then in the first place? Who forced you
to? Were you dragged here by the scruff of your neck?
That's right—take an expensive apartment with no money
to pay for it. And now, of course, you don't know which
way to turn! Oh, I know, I know . . . and after getting used
to spacious surroundings you'll have to come down and
live in one room with bare boards and an oil store. You'll
enjoy that, won't you?

GLOUMOV. Well, as a matter of fact, I'm planning to move to
a bigger apartment.

MAMAEV. A bigger one! You haven't got the means to keep
up this and you want to take a bigger one. Are you quite
right in the head? Is that the reason?

GLOUMOV. No, I don't think so. . . . It's just stupidity.

MAMAEV. Stupidity, what nonsense!

GLOUMOV. I wish it were, but I'm just plain stupid.

MAMAEV. Stupid, that's funny. In what way stupid?

GLOUMOV. I'm a bit simple . . . not enough brains. There's
nothing funny in that, is there? It's quite usual.

MAMAEV. Now this is very interesting—a man accuses himself of being stupid.

GLOUMOV. Well, it comes better from me than other people. I mean I'd rather say it first. It's no use my trying to hide it.

MAMAEV. Yes, of course, it's rather difficult to hide a defect like that.

GLOUMOV. I never try to.

MAMAEV, *shaking his head.* Tch, tch, tch, very sad, most regrettable.

GLOUMOV *inclines his head.*

There's no one to teach you, to guide you, I suppose?

GLOUMOV. No one.

MAMAEV. But there *are* teachers. Very intelligent teachers, but nobody listens to them these days. Of course, you can't expect much from the old folks. Most of them imagine just because they're old, they must be intelligent and in no need of instruction—but when the youngsters won't listen to you either, well, what's the world coming to? Take one case for instance, I stopped a schoolboy who was rushing away from school. "Yes," I said, "you rush out of school fast enough, but it's a different story hen you're going to school in the morning. You creep along slowly enough then, I'll be bound." Well, you'd think any decent boy would be grateful that a man of my standing should bother to stop in the street and talk to him, but not a bit of it with this young puppy. Instead of kissing my hand as you'd expect, do you know what he said?

GLOUMOV. No.

MAMAEV. "Save your lectures for your fat wife," he said. Then he stuck out his tongue, called out a rude name and ran off.

GLOUMOV. Disgusting! . . . Well, poor lad, I suppose he'd got no one to set his footsteps on the right path.

MAMAEV. Exactly. Do you know why servants are so bad nowadays? Because they no longer have to look to their masters for instruction and guidance. In the old days I used to advise my employees on the conduct of every detail of their lives. I used to lecture them all—from the highest to the lowest. I used to spend about two hours on every one of them giving them instructions. I used to rise to the very highest spheres of thought and there he'd be standing in front of me—so overcome that by the time I'd finished he'd be worn out with sighing. It was good for him and a noble occupation for me. But all that's changed now—since the great calamity. You know what I'm referring to?

GLOUMOV. The freeing of the serfs?

MAMAEV, *shaking his head and drawing his breath between his teeth.* The worst thing that ever happened to this country. You try lecturing a servant these days. You give him one or two lectures on metaphysics or something exalted and he goes and gives notice. "What's this a punishment for?" he says. "I haven't done anything." Yes, a punishment he calls it—a punishment!

GLOUMOV. Oh, it's wicked, really wicked!

MAMAEV. You know, I'm not a stern man, I do it all with words. Not like some of these nouveau riche gentlemen. When they have to reprimand a servant they catch hold of him by the hair and pull it at every word. I've seen them. He understands it better that way, they say. Makes it more comprehensible. Well, that's not my method. Do it all with words, I say, but do you think they're grateful to me? Not a bit of it.

GLOUMOV. Yes, it must be heart-breaking for you.

MAMAEV. Heart-breaking? Every time I think about it it's like a knife going through me here.
Pressing his hand to his chest.

GLOUMOV. Where did you say a knife was going through you?
Indicating on his own chest.
Here?

MAMAEV. No, no, not there. Here.

GLOUMOV. What, here?

MAMAEV. No, higher up. Look . . . here.

GLOUMOV. Oh, I see. Here.

MAMAEV. No, no, not there at all. Higher up I tell you.

GLOUMOV. Do forgive me. I told you I was stupid.

MAMAEV. Yes, I'm afraid you are. . . . It's a very great disadvantage but it can be overcome if you've elderly, experienced friends or relations to advise you.

GLOUMOV. That's just the trouble. I haven't anyone like that. There's my mother, of course, but she's even more stupid than I am.

MAMAEV. Tch, tch, tch, it's a very bad position for a young man to be in.

GLOUMOV. I *have* got an uncle in Moscow, at least, he's really only a cousin but I think of him as my uncle——

MAMAEV. Well, can't you go to him?

GLOUMOV. I wish I could. I hear he can give invaluable advice out of his great fund of knowledge and experience. But he doesn't even know of my existence and nothing would induce me to scrape acquaintance with him.

MAMAEV. That's a most regrettable attitude to take.

GLOUMOV. Oh, you misunderstand me! If he were poor like myself I'd kneel in front of him, I'd kiss the hem of his garment. But he's rich, he's a great man in Moscow. If I were to go and ask for his advice he'd think I'd come for money. How could I explain that I didn't want a farthing from him, that all I wanted as the help and guidance that he alone could give me, that I'm thirsting and starving for those divine words of guidance, for some heavenly lecture that would drop from his lips like manna from heaven! . . . Oh, if he were only poor and I could meet him, I'd listen to him day and night!

MAMAEV. Mmm. . . . You don't appear to be as stupid as you say.

GLOUMOV. Yes, at times lucid moments come over me—a fog seems to clear from my brain, but only for a second; most of the time I feel as if I'm not quite all there. That's where I need someone to advise me.

MAMAEV. And who is this cousin—this uncle?

GLOUMOV. I hardly remember his name. I think it's, um . . . it's Mamaev; I think. Neel Fedoseitch Mamaev.

MAMAEV. Mamaev! . . . And may I ask what is your name?

GLOUMOV. Gloumov. Yegor Gloumov.

MAMAEV. Dmitri Gloumov's son?

GLOUMOV. Yes.

MAMAEV. Well, God bless my soul, what an extraordinary thing!

GLOUMOV. Did you know my father?

MAMAEV. Why I am that very Neel Fedoseitch Mamaev that you're speaking of.

GLOUMOV. *What?*

MAMAEV. Yes, it's me—it's I—it's me!

GLOUMOV. Oh good heavens! You're Uncle Mamaev! I can hardly believe it! Oh uncle, you *will* let me call you uncle, won't you?
Almost in tears.
Please let me take your hand, let me look at you. Oh, but uncle, I've heard you don't like your relations. I quite understand you must know so many wonderful people, but don't worry, I shall never intrude on you. It's quite enough for me that I've seen you in the flesh and talked to you. I shall never forget what you've said to me. The wonderful advice you've given me today.

MAMAEV. My dear boy, whenever you want advice about anything come to me.

GLOUMOV. But I *always* need it, uncle, always.

MAMAEV. Well, there you are. Come in tonight.

GLOUMOV. Oh, how can I ever thank you! But I must break the wonderful news to Mamma. Do you think I might present her to you?

MAMAEV. Well, why not? Fetch her in.

GLOUMOV, *calling out.* Mamma! She's not very brilliant I'm afraid, but she's got a heart of gold.

MADAME GLOUMOVA *comes in. Going to her.*

Mamma, darling, what *do* you think, only you must promise me not to cry.

To MAMAEV.

It may be too much for her.

Turning to his mother again.

Who do you think has turned up? It's Papa's dear second cousin, Mr. Mamaev—for years Mamma's been longing to meet you.

To MADAME GLOUMOVA *again.*

Isn't it wonderful, Mamma, and he's going to let me call him uncle.

MADAME G. Indeed, I've always longed to see him.

Coming down to MAMAEV.

I've heard so much about you from dear Dmitri, my sainted husband, God rest his soul. Why you were almost the last person he spoke of before he passed away, do you remember, Yegor? . . . And to think God has sent you to us at last. *Weeps.*

MAMAEV. ⎫ Come now, you mustn't take it like this.

GLOUMOV. ⎭ Mamma, darling, you promised not to cry.

MADAME G., *through her tears.* Oh no, I can't help it. I know it's stupid of me. . . . But they say that uncle doesn't like his relations. God has sent him to us and now he'll snatch himself away again.

MAMAEV. No need to get upset. After all, there are relations and relations.

MADAME G., *wiping her nose and drying her eyes.* You must forgive me, it's the shock coming so suddenly like this. . . . But let me look at you, dear Neel Fedoseitch. Dmitri's own second cousin! . . . But Yegor, he's not a bit like it.

During the ensuing scene, STYOPKA *enters and unobtrusively lays the table for a meal.*

GLOUMOV, *in a hoarse whisper.* Mamma!

He nudges her violently.

MADAME G. What's the matter? He isn't like it, is he, you can't say he is.

MAMAEV. What is all this? Who is it I'm not like?

GLOUMOV, *to* MADAME GLOUMOVA. Why must you blurt things out like this? Don't listen, uncle, she's only talking nonsense.

MAMAEV. Oh no, one must tell the whole story or nothing at all.

MADAME G. I'm simply saying that the portrait isn't a bit like you.

MAMAEV. What portrait? Where have you got a portrait from?

MADAME G. Well you see, Yegor Kourchaev comes to see us sometimes. He's a nephew of yours too, isn't he?

GLOUMOV. Such a charming fellow.

MAMAEV. Yes? well, and what?

MADAME G. He happened to draw a picture of you. Yegor, show it to uncle.

GLOUMOV. Oh, Mamma! I really don't know where I put it.

MADAME G. Oh well, do find it. He was drawing it just now, you remember, and who was that with him, that peculiar man, you know, who writes rude rhymes about people? Kourchaev said, "I'll draw a picture of my uncle for you and you write something underneath." I was in the room, I heard them.

MAMAEV. Show me this picture. Show it to me!

GLOUMOV, *handing it to him.* Mamma, you really ought to be more discreet!

MAMAEV. That's right, teach your mother to be a hypocrite.
Looks at the picture.
What's this, a—a hippopotamus? What's it say underneath?

GLOUMOV, *looking over his shoulder.* Uncle Mamaev, the talking hippopotamus.

MADAME G. Talking hippopotamus, that's it.
A pause.

MAMAEV, *suddenly crumpling the picture up in his fist.* If that young man dares to show his face in my house again, I—I'll teach him! So that's gratitude, after all I've done, young blackguard! I've advised him, I've lectured him, I've tried

to put him on the right path. Well, thank the lord my eyes
have been opened anyway. . . .

To GLOUMOV.

Do you draw libellous portraits of me, young man?

GLOUMOV. Oh uncle, please, what do you take me for?

MAMAEV. Well, you must come round this evening without
fail. I shall expect you, and you too, Madame Gloumova.

MADAME G. Oh no, let Yegor go alone. I'm sure you don't want
me to come, boring you with my nonsense.

MAMAEV. Not at all, my wife will be delighted.
He makes for the door, GLOUMOV *following.* MAMAEV'S
servant holds the door open for them.

GLOUMOV. Mamma and I will look forward to it. What time
will you expect us then?

MAMAEV. Any time after eight o'clock.

GLOUMOV. What a wonderful chance your coming here today.
At door.
Good-bye, uncle.

MAMAEV. Good-bye. Don't come before eight or we shan't
have finished supper.
Calling out to servant as he goes toward the stairs.
Come on, hurry up. Don't stand there gaping like a half-wit!
Servant hurries after him.

GLOUMOV. Good-bye, Uncle.
He half closes the door and turns to the others. STYOPKA
bursts into peals of long-suppressed laughter. GLOUMOV
*comes back into the room. He speaks jubilantly, signing
to* STYOPKA *to be quiet.*
It's working, it's working—everything's working according
to plan!

STYOPKA, *doubled up with merriment.* Oh! . . . the old codger's
face when he saw the hippopotamus! I thought I'd burst,
I really did.

MADAME G. Be quiet, can't you? He'll hear you on the stairs.
Dolt!

STYOPKA. I said he'd soon have us all on our feet in a fine mansion again, didn't I?

MADAME G. Don't put the smoked herring on the table like that. Put it on a plate properly.

GLOUMOV. Mamma, you were very helpful indeed about the picture. Thank you.
Embraces her.

MADAME G., *modestly.* Oh well, I was only doing my best.

GLOUMOV. Come on, let's begin, I'm hungry.
All three seat themselves at the table.

MADAME G. This must have cost a few roubles.

GLOUMOV. It's all right. He got it on Kourchaev's account.

MADAME G. Good. Open the wine, Styopka.

GLOUMOV. Better call Madame Maniefa in.

MADAME G. She's asleep, let's leave her. She'd put me off my food.

STYOPKA. The old gentleman's face when he saw the hippopotamus!
Imitating him.
"If that young man dares to show his face in my house again!"
They all choke with laughter.
KOURCHAEV *bursts in at the front door. He is pale and trembling with fury.*

KOURCHAEV. Has my uncle been here?
They stop laughing abruptly. All three turn and look at him, then STYOPKA *jumps up and pretends to be waiting at table.*

GLOUMOV. Yes, why? And do you mind knocking before you come in?

KOURCHAEV. Have you been discussing me with him?

GLOUMOV. Discussing you? Why should I be? He just came in to see the apartment.

KOURCHAEV, *advancing into the room.* I don't believe it, do you hear me? It's a plot, that's what it is. It's some devilish plot against me.

MADAME G. Don't raise your voice in front of me, please.

KOURCHAEV. I'm sorry but I can't control myself. I ran into my uncle in the street just now and he told me he never wanted to see my face again. Can you imagine that?

GLOUMOV. I'm imagining it. Can you imagine it, Mamma?

KOURCHAEV. I go to Madame Tourousina's and she refuses to see me—sends up one of her so-called companions, one of those disgusting hangers-on of hers to forbid me the house! Do you hear what I'm saying?

GLOUMOV. Yes, I hear.

KOURCHAEV. I demand an explanation of it!

GLOUMOV. Why come to me for an explanation? If you want to know I should think the explanation's in the sort of life you lead.

KOURCHAEV. It's no different from any other fellow's Whatever I may have done, it's no reason to—break off a fellow's engagement to a girl, to take a fellow's legacy away.

GLOUMOV. And what about your friends? Golutvin for instance.

KOURCHAEV. Golutvin?

GLOUMOV. Yes, Golutvin!
Springing to his feet.
How dare you bring that creature to this house?! How dare you introduce him to my mother!

MADAME G. Yes, how dare you!

GLOUMOV. I happen to be particular about the people I mix with. I must protect Mamma and myself against the recurrence of such an incident, therefore I ask you kindly not to visit us again.

MADAME G. I should think not!

KOURCHAEV, *to* GLOUMOV. Have you gone mad?

GLOUMOV. Mr. Mamaev's thought it fit to turn you out and I wish to follow his example, that's all. Styopka, show this gentleman the door.

KOURCHAEV. All right, all right, I'm going. But let me tell you this, if this is your work, my fine fellow, if my suspicions prove correct, you'd better look out. I'm warning you, take care, that's all.

GLOUMOV. I shall take care when it's necessary, but at the moment I see no serious danger.

STYOPKA. This way, sir.

Holding the door open.

KOURCHAEV *glares at* GLOUMOV *for a second, then turns on his heel and marches out.* STYOPKA *closes the door, bursting into raucous laughter again.* GLOUMOV *and his mother join in, then still laughing start to pile into the food.* STYOPKA *sits at the table again and helps himself.* MANIEFA *appears, the empty vodka bottle in her hand and a tipsy smile on her face. She moves unsteadily to the table.*

Curtain.

ACT ONE

SCENE 2

The MAMAEVS' *house. A conservatory. At the back is a door leading to the ballroom, which is obscured by palms, ferns and trellis-work. A ball is in progress and gay music can be heard throughout the scene. Two elderly gentlemen are heard.*

MAMAEV, *off.* Yes, we are going somewhere, we're being led towards something or other;

Entering, followed by KROUTITZKY.

but neither we nor those who are leading us know whither we're going, or what we're going to do when we get there.

KROUTITZKY *is as tall, thin, pallid and distinguished, as* MAMAEV *is short, red-faced, fat and commonplace.* MAMAEV *has a plate of "refreshments" which he is eating with his fingers.*

KROUTITZKY. The younger generation can't settle down. They want to alter everything: let's try this, let's try that, I'll alter this, I'll change that. It's easy enough to change anything. The furniture in this conservatory for instance, I can take it and I can stand it upside down— there's change for you: but what of the centuries of wisdom, of experience, which lie behind the making of a table with four legs to stand on? There stands a table on four legs and does it stand firmly?

MAMAEV. Firm as a rock.

Places his hand on it. It wobbles.

Oh, something's wrong with the leg.

Bending down and peering at the leg.

It needs a wedge underneath.

KROUTITZKY. That's beside the point. Now we'll take the table and we'll turn it upside down.

They do so.

There you are, you see, we've done it.

MAMAEV, *proudly surveying their handiwork.* That's it, we've done it.

KROUTITZKY. So much for change.

Sitting down, they contemplate the upturned table. KROUTITZKY *adds.*

Or we could lay it sideways.

MAMAEV *gets up.*

No, no, upside down is more telling. This should show the younger generation what their passion for change will lead to.

MAMAEV. But will they see?

KROUTITZKY. Well, if they don't they must be taught to see. There are people capable of teaching after all!

MAMAEV. Yes, I know there are, but the tragedy of it is they won't listen. They don't want to listen to men of intelligence and wisdom.

KROUTITZKY. It's our own fault. We may know how to express our opinions in words but that's not enough. We should write them. Only the young people write nowadays. That's the answer to the problem. One must write more, write, write.

MAMAEV. It's all very well to say write, but you've got to have the knack of it. One may be the most intelligent man in Moscow and yet not have that particular knack. Take myself for instance: I can express myself in words. If you asked me to I could start talking now and continue till this time tomorrow, but if you asked me to write—I couldn't do it, merely because I haven't got the knack. . . . Have you got the knack?

KROUTITZY. Oh yes, I write a great deal.

MAMAEV. Ah well, I suppose some people are born with it.

KROUTITZKY. The time has gone when a command of language is sufficient to make oneself felt. In these days one must have command over the pen.

MAMAEV. Yes, but suppose one lacks the knack. It's not a question of intelligence.

KROUTITZKY. Oh no, no, I wasn't suggesting such a thing. . . . By the way, do you happen to know of a young man, fairly well-educated, of fairly good family, who could express on paper ideas, thoughts, plans for the improvement of the Russian people, for instance?

MAMAEV. Yes. I know exactly the young fellow you want.

KROUTITZKY. He mustn't be one of these frivolous, free-thinking young men one finds today, always gossiping and turning everything to ridicule.

MAMAEV. Not in the least! But I'll present him to you later.

KROUTITZKY. Is he here now—in the ballroom?

MAMAEV. He's not turned up yet.

KROUTITZKY. The truth is I've worked out a very important Plan for the Improvement of the Russian Peoples. Well, as you know, I'm a man who's been educated in the old school.

MAMAEV. And a far, far better one, too.

KROUTITZKY. So naturally I express myself in the old style, the—how shall I describe it—well, if I may say so, in the style of the great Lomonosoff.

MAMAEV. Ah, Lomonosoff, yes, the Russian Shakespeare!

KROUTITZKY. Not at all. Shakespeare was the English Lomono-soff. But as I was saying, if one writes nowadays in the style of Lomonosoff or Sumarokoff one would only be laughed at; so do you think this young friend of ours might, well, slightly rewrite my work for me in the less eloquent language of today?

MAMAEV. I don't see why not.

KROUTITZKY. I should pay him adequately, of course.

MAMAEV. Even if you gave him too little, he'd consider it an honor.

KROUTITZKY. I wouldn't care to be under an obligation to him, er—what did you say his name was? .

MAMAEV. My cousin, my dear cousin, Yegor Dimitrich Gloumov.

MADAME MAMAEV *hurries in from the ballroom followed by* MADAME GLOUMOVA. KLEOPATRA IVOVNA MAMAEVA *is a woman in her forties, over-dressed in a style too young for her, exceedingly vain and making much coy play with her fan.*

KLEOPATRA, *as she enters.* He has everything one hopes to find in a young man, charm good manners, looks.

Seeing MAMAEV *and* KROUTITZKY.

Oh, you two naughty men! Boring each other in here. You should be entertaining the guests. Yegor and dear cousin Glafira have arrived. Let me present you—Glafira Gloumova —Mr. Kroutitzky.

MADAME G., *as* KROUTITZKY *takes her hand.* I'm quite be-wildered at so much splendour—so many distinguished gen-tlemen, but it's always the same at Cousin Kleopatra's.

Turning to MAMAEV.

I've a bone to pick with you, dear Neel Fedoseitch.

MAMAEV. What about?

MADAME G. You're taking my son away from me. He doesn't love his poor old mother any more. It's uncle this, uncle that, "nobody's as clever as uncle" he says.

MAMAEV. He's a good boy, a good boy.

KLEOPATRA. And so charming, so modest. He doesn't want to dance with any of the young girls in the ballroom. He's quite content just to sit and watch or to talk to his auntie.

KROUTITZKY *to* MAMAEV. Is this the young man you were speaking of?

MAMAEV, *leading the way to the ballroom.* Come in and meet him.

MADAME G., *following them, determined to get a few more words in.* He was always the same, even as a tiny boy. He'd never forget to kiss Papa and Mamma good night.
MAMAEV and KROUTITZKY *are forced to stop and listen to her. She continues.*
And he'd kiss all his grandmammas and grandpapas good night too, and even great aunt Eudoxia Gregorovna he'd kiss, although she had a big wart and quite a long moustache. I shall never forget one morning, he put his little head round the door, "Mamma," he said, "I dweamt about ve angels las' night. Two ever such booful angels flew wite up to my cot and vey said, Love papa and mamma and obey vem in everyfing and never forget when you gwow up always love your elders and betters and obey vem too. And I said fank you, fank you, booful angels and I'll always obey evwebody." I can see it as if it were yesterday, with his little head poking round the door and his lovely long ringlets hanging round his face.

KLEOPATRA. Oh, the darling pet!

MAMAEV. I'm very pleased with your son. You can tell him that. I'm very pleased with him.
He follows KROUTITZKY *who goes into the ballroom, then coming back to* MADAME GLOUMOVA *says, confidentially.*
I know your husband's death left you in a bad way. Tell you what, you come and see me one morning, and I'll give you some. . . .

MADAME G. Oh, it's too kind of you. I couldn't take it.

MAMAEV. Not money. Something much better. Advice. You bring your household accounts to me. I'll go through them and see what items you can cut out.
He goes into the ballroom.

MADAME G. Oh, you're too good to us, dear Kleopatra. If it hadn't been for you, poor Yegor would have lived out all his life in obscurity—never going anywhere or meeting anyone.

KLEOPATRA. Oh, but we'd have been bound to notice him some time or other.

MADAME G. I don't see why. You have to be clever for people to notice you.

KLEOPATRA. Not at all. There's no need for a great brain when you're as handsome as Yegor. What does he want a brain for, he's not going to be a professor. A good-looking young man can always find somebody who'll help him simply out of sympathy. Either to make a career or just with money so that he can live comfortably. With a clever man it's different. Nobody minds if they see a clever man shabbily dressed, living in a cheap apartment and dining off a cold sausage and a piece of bread—that doesn't bring a lump to your throat and make you feel you must do something for him. You expect a clever man to live like that. But when you see a poor boy who's young and handsome, shabbily dressed, then it's unbearable. It mustn't be allowed, no, and it won't be, never. I'll see that it isn't!

MADAME G. What an angel you are. An angel!

KLEOPATRA. The women of Moscow must band together! We must insist that our friends, our husbands, all the authorities rise to their feet to help him. We simply cannot allow a handsome young man to be spoilt by poverty. There are so few of them nowadays. Of course, we should sympathise with all poor people, it's our duty, that goes without saying —but to see a handsome young man with sleeves too short, or frayed shirt collars, that's what touches the heart! And besides a man can't be bold and dashing when he's poor, he can't have that conquering expression, that air of jauntiness which is so pardonable in a handsome young man.

MADAME G. Yegor's so grateful to you, dear Kleopatra. And no one knows how to be grateful better than he does.

KLEOPATRA. That's very pleasant to hear.

MADAME G. It's more than gratitude even. He positively adores you both.

KLEOPATRA. Adores? . . . Aren't you exaggerating?

MADAME G. Not a bit. It's part of his character, his beautiful soul. Of course, it's not for me to praise my own son and he hates my talking about him, but—

KLEOPATRA. Oh, please go on. I promise not to tell.

MADAME G. Well, there's no one in the world like you two, he thinks. Neel Fedoseitch's brain, well you know what he thinks about that, but your beauty—well, he says it's indescribable. It should be immortalised on canvas.

KLEOPATRA. Oh, really! . . . Did he really say that?

MADAME G. And shall I tell you something else he said to me —no, perhaps I hadn't better.

KLEOPATRA. *Do* go on, please. What was it he said?

MADAME G. Well, promise not to be angry with me.

KLEOPATRA. No, no, of course not.

MADAME G. I'm so stupid, I always blurt everything out.

KLEOPATRA, *eagerly.* Yes, yes, what was it he said?

MADAME G. Well, "Auntie's an angel," he said to me one day. "An angel," and all at once he put his head on my bosom and burst into tears.

KLEOPATRA. Oh! . . . Whatever made him do that? . . . How strange. . . . What else did he say?

MADAME G., *hesitantly.* It's . . . it's not so much what Yegor said in words, but dear Kleopatra, do forgive him, he's only a young man and you know what young men are. I'm afraid he has a passionate nature—how can I explain? . . . He's like a volcano underneath, and ever since he's met you, well, I'm frightened all the time that any moment he might erupt.

KLEOPATRA, *faintly.* Oh! . . . Do you think he might?

MADAME G. Oh dear, I'm afraid I've said too much and spoilt everything, but . . . whatever he feels for you it's purely as a relation. . . . And yet, one has to admit at his age the proximity of a beautiful woman—well he never sleeps a wink at night after seeing you . . . I can hear him tossing and turning.

KLEOPATRA. Tell me. . . . Does he confide in you? . . . Or does he hide his very deepest feelings?

MADAME G. From his mamma? Never! He's just like a little boy, he tells me everything.

KLEOPATRA. Yes . . . a little boy . . . but like a volcano, too. What he wants is an experienced woman to guide him.

MADAME G., *fervently*. Oh, couldn't it be you!

KLEOPATRA, *laughs delightedly*. You're very fond of him, I can see that.

MADAME G. Fond? He's my only child.
As though carried away.
I love him, I love him!

KLEOPATRA, *taking her hand*. We must love him together.

MADAME G. We must! We will!
They embrace. MADAME GLOUMOVA *apparently recovering from overwhelming emotion, blows her nose.*
I don't know what Yegor would say if he knew I'd told you all this. You'll never let him know, will you? Promise?

KLEOPATRA. Darling, never, never.
Clasping her hands.

MADAME G. Only, you see, he feels quite ashamed of his poor old mother sometimes because she's so stupid. I know he does.

GLOUMOV, *entering from the ballroom.* Oh!
As though taken aback at seeing KLEOPATRA.
I was looking for Mamma. I didn't know you were with her, auntie.

KLEOPATRA. Come in, come in. There's nothing to be afraid of. Why so shy still?

GLOUMOV. If you and Mamma are talking. . . .

MADAME G. Auntie's had quite enough of my foolish nonsense,

I'm sure. Kleopatra, dear, let me get you some refreshments.
You've been so busy with your guests you've had nothing.
She makes for the door.

KLEOPATRA. No, no thank you. How thoughtful you are. Get
yourself something, darling.

MADAME G. Don't you worry about silly old mother.

To GLOUMOV.

You mustn't be so bashful, dear. Stay and talk to auntie.
You must learn how to behave with young, beautiful ladies,
mustn't he, Kleopatra? . . . But you'll soon learn; auntie
will teach you. . . .

She goes out.

A pause. KLEOPATRA *waits for him to speak but he stands
bashfully in front of her like a schoolboy.*

KLEOPATRA. Come. Sit down next to me.

He does so awkwardly.

You must be more free and easy in your manner. After all,
I'm only a human being like everybody else, am I not?

GLOUMOV. Yes, Auntie.

KLEOPATRA, *tapping with her fan.* And don't call me auntie
all the time.

GLOUMOV. May I really call you—Kleopatra?

KLEOPATRA. Of course, silly boy—and why aren't you more
open with me?

GLOUMOV. Open?

KLEOPATRA. Yes. I feel that something's worrying you. I see a
wild look in your eyes sometimes. Couldn't you tell me what
it is? I might be able to help you.

GLOUMOV. Oh, if only I could! If only you were——

KLEOPATRA. Were what?

GLOUMOV. A middle-aged woman.

KLEOPATRA. But I don't want to be a middle-aged woman.

GLOUMOV, *with sudden passion.* The very thought of it's unbearable! What I mean is if you weren't so young and beautiful I wouldn't feel so shy.

KLEOPATRA. Now sit closer and tell me everything frankly. Why wouldn't you be so shy if I were a middle-aged woman?

GLOUMOV. A young woman has her own affairs, her own interests, she's no time for bothering about her poor relations! Whereas a middle-aged woman has nothing else to do.

KLEOPATRA. And why can't a young woman take an interest in her relations?

GLOUMOV. She can, but one wouldn't like to ask her. One's afraid of boring her. Her life's full of gaiety and amusement. The last thing in the world she wants to see is some dull nephew or cousin with a long face, always importuning her with tedious requests. With a middle-aged woman, it would be different. She'd have a new interest in life. She'd enjoy bustling about Moscow using her influence for him, and letting all her friends know what a kind heart she had.

KLEOPATRA. Well, suppose I were a middle-aged woman, what would you ask me to do for you?

GLOUMOV. But you're not, you're a very young woman. You're trying to catch me.

KLEOPATRA. Well, it's all the same. Go on—suppose I were middle-aged just for the sake of argument.

GLOUMOV. It's not all the same but—well, for instance, I know you'd only have to say one word to Ivan Gorodoulin and I should get a good post in the Civil Service.

KLEOPATRA. Yes, one word to Gorodoulin would be enough.

GLOUMOV. But I wouldn't bother you with such a tedious request.

KLEOPATRA. Why not?

GLOUMOV. To begin with, it wouldn't be fair to ask him.

KLEOPATRA. Not fair, why?

GLOUMOV. Because he's in love with you.

KLEOPATRA. What makes you think that?

GLOUMOV. I'm certain of it.

KLEOPATRA. What a lot you know! And can you tell me what I feel towards him?

GLOUMOV. Only you know that.

KLEOPATRA. Aren't you . . . interested in what I feel?

GLOUMOV. It's not for me to pry into your secret feelings.

KLEOPATRA. Well, what would *you* feel if you thought that I returned his passion?

GLOUMOV, *after hesitating.* I only know this, there's nothing Gorodoulin dare refuse you. He'd be delighted if you asked a favor of him so to make you ask him for something for me would be like giving him a bribe.

KLEOPATRA. Sheer imagination! So you don't want me to speak about you?

GLOUMOV. Positively not. I couldn't let myself be indebted to you. What could I do to repay you?

KLEOPATRA. How would you repay—a middle-aged woman?

GLOUMOV. Oh, that would be simple! I should pander to her, indulge her whims, carry her dog, push the footstool towards her, keep kissing her hand and telling her she didn't look a day over twenty-five. But unless she were middle-aged, there'd be no point in all that.

KLEOPATRA. No, of course not.

GLOUMOV. And I daresay I'd soon become very attached to her if she were kind and charming. Really fond of her, in fact.

KLEOPATRA. But couldn't you become fond of a young woman?

GLOUMOV. I could, but I wouldn't dare to!

KLEOPATRA, *behind her fan.* At last! . . .

GORODOULIN *appears in the door of the ballroom. He is a man of thirty-five or so, consciously sophisticated.*

GORODOULIN. Am I intruding?

KLEOPATRA, *starting but quickly recovering herself.* Come in,

Ivan. I was thinking of you only a moment ago. Let me present my cousin, Yegor Dimitrich Gloumov—Ivan Ivanovitch Gorodoulin.

The two men bow.

Yegor, be a dear boy and fetch me a glass of wine.

Fanning herself.

It's insufferably hot tonight.

As YEGOR *reaches the door, his mother appears carrying some refreshments and peering into the conservatory with an eager, crafty expression. Unseen by the others, he intercepts her, pushing her back into the ballroom in front of him.*

KLEOPATRA.Why pursue me in here when there are so many eligible young ladies to dance with?

GORODOULIN. I can't even see them. I may appear calm, Kleopatra, but there's a tumult in my brain and a storm of passion in my heart.

KLEOPATRA. That's very nice of you. I'm very glad I'm not entirely forgotten—poor, lonely, neglected me.

GORODOULIN. Who is this man who dares to neglect you? Is he here? Point him out to me, that's all. I'm in a particularly pugnacious mood today.

KLEOPATRA. You're the principal culprit. It's you who deserve to be shot—or at least punished in some way.

GORODOULIN. At your fair hands, lady, I don't mind which.

KLEOPATRA. I've already thought of a punishment for you.

GORODOULIN. What is it? To be strangled in your embrace?

KLEOPATRA. No, I'm going to ask a favour of you.

GORODOULIN. Oh, I see, you wish to reverse our roles.

KLEOPATRA. What do you mean?

GORODOULIN. You wish to come to me in the humble role of a petitioner.

KLEOPATRA. Are you a petitioner? I thought you were a judge or likely to become one, one day.

GORODOULIN. Yes, but with women I'm always——

KLEOPATRA. Do stop being fatuous. I've serious business to discuss.

GORODOULIN. I'm all attention.

KLEOPATRA. My nephew is badly in need of a——

GORODOULIN. Of a what? A new school uniform, some white mice?

KLEOPATRA. Oh, don't be tiresome. Listen to me and don't interrupt. He's not really my nephew, he's my cousin—the young man you've just met and he's very charming, intelligent, and good-looking.

GORODOULIN. So much the worse for me.

KLEOPATRA. He wants a job.

GORODOULIN. What do you fancy for him?

KLEOPATRA. An important job in the Civil Service. He's extremely capable.

GORODOULIN. In that case they wouldn't want him.

KLEOPATRA. I shall become very bored with you in a moment and we shall quarrel. Do you know of a post for him?

GORODOULIN. Well, I might know of something for an ordinary young man: for a paragon of intelligence, I should find it difficult. Let's have a look at this phenomenon, and I'll tell you what I could recommend him for.

KLEOPATRA, *as* GLOUMOV *comes in.* Thank you, Yegor.
Getting up and going towards him.
How kind of you.
Taking the wine he's brought her.
Now I shall leave you two men together. I'm neglecting my guests.
Raising her glass.
Here's to your friendship. . . . I shall come back in a little while and see how you've got on.

GLOUMOV, *opening the door for her.* Allow me.

She gives him a languishing glance and goes out. He turns to GORODOULIN.

What a charming woman my cousin is.

GORODOULIN, *without enthusiasm.* Yes, charming, charming.
A pause.
Ever been in the Civil Service?

GLOUMOV, *jauntily.* I was once but I gave it up.

GORODOULIN. Why?

GLOUMOV. I hadn't the qualifications for the job. Whatever
qualities I may have, they're not much use there.

GORODOULIN. Surely all one needs is an average brain and the
ability to work a few hours a day.

GLOUMOV. I wouldn't say I was lacking in either of those qualities, but are they likely to get one anywhere? They might
be enough if one's content to finish one's life as a petty
government official. If you're to go on without influence
some very different qualities are necessary.

GORODOULIN. What, for instance?

GLOUMOV. One must be able to keep one's reasoning powers
in abeyance unless specifically ordered to use them, to
laugh loudly but not too loudly, when one's boss unbends
enough to make a joke, to do all the thinking for one's su-
periors as well as all the work for them, at the same time
giving the impression that you're unutterably stupid and
that they've thought of everything themselves. Besides
this, you must have several sycophantic qualities which
at the same time mustn't be too obvious; for instance, as
soon as your boss enters the office you must jump to your
feet and spring to attention in a way that's both obsequious
and yet not obsequious, cringing and yet at the same time
noble and trustworthy. Then when he sends you for something you must tear off to get it but without giving the impression of an undignified rush. Something between a
mazurka, a gallop, and a goose step.

GORODOULIN, *laughing.* You put it most amusingly. But it
doesn't hold good still. Things have changed in the last
few years.

GLOUMOV. I don't see any difference. It's all papers and forms, the entire Civil Service is like a fortress made of papers, forms, and red tape. The unfortunate ciitzens of Moscow have to cower before it under an incessant bombardment of circulars, orders, forms, and certificates.

GORODOULIN. Do you realise that you've a considerable talent for expressing things?

GLOUMOV. I'm so glad you sympathise with my ideas. There aren't many people who would.

GORODOULIN. It's not the ideas! Anyone can have ideas. It's the wording, the phrasing that's good. Would you do me a very great favour?

GLOUMOV. Of course. What?

GORODOULIN. Write all that down on paper.

GLOUMOV. Of course, if you want it—but what for?

GORODOULIN. I'll be quite frank with you. I wouldn't dream of telling this to anybody else, but you and I understand each other. We are both men of principle, we can be completely open. The trouble is I've got to make an after-dinner speech tomorrow and I simply haven't had the time to think.

GLOUMOV. Well, of course I'll help you.

GORODOULIN, *patting his hand.* Do this for me as a friend.

GLOUMOV. Don't say another word about it. No, you give me a job where I can be of some use to my fellow men, where I can study them—study their daily needs and see that they're satisfied promptly and sympathetically.

GORODOULIN. That's wonderful, really wonderful! Would you mind writing that down too. . . . Now I think the best post for an honest, idealistic man like yourself would be as head of some State philanthropical institution.

GLOUMOV. I don't mind what work I do as long as it would be useful and constructive, would augment the quantity of good necessary for the well-being of the masses.

GORODOULIN. I say, would you write that down too? "To augment the quantity of good——" that's very fine indeed.

GLOUMOV. Would you like me to write the whole speech for you?

GORODOULIN. Would you really? There you are, you see, we've only spoken a few words and we're friends in no time. Simply because we share the same principles and ideas.

Glancing at his watch.

I'd better go back and have a word with Kleopatra. Poor soul, she will give these insufferable receptions; she's the only one who enjoys them and one spends the evening waiting on and flattering her because one can't afford to fall out with the old man. . . .

Going towards the ballroom.

Are you coming?

GLOUMOV. Not for a moment.

GORODOULIN. But you talk so well, my dear fellow! We need men like you in Moscow! A pity there aren't more like you. *He goes.*

Left to himself GLOUMOV *produces a notebook and writes in it.*

MADAME G., *putting her head round the door, then coming into the conservatory carrying a plate of caviar with which she is stuffing herself. She says conspiratorially.* Oh, you're alone. How did everything go? What did she say?

GLOUMOV. I can't tell you now, Mamma. Don't interrupt me.

MADAME G. What are you doing?

GLOUMOV. Making notes for my diary. I must put everything down while it's fresh in my mind.

MADAME G., *peering over his shoulder.* Have you put down everything she said to you? This caviar's delicious. I've got four pots in my bag to take home.

GLOUMOV. Do leave me alone, Mamma.

MAMAEVA *comes in.*

MAMAEV. Just the man I'm looking for.

MADAME G. Oh, I won't disturb you if you two want to talk. *Scuttling out.*

Go on, go on, don't take any notice of me. Silly old mother, always in the way.

GLOUMOV. Yes, Uncle?

MAMAEV. Here, come here.

Mysteriously.

I've been talking to Kroutitzky; he wanted my advice on a certain matter. Very decent old fellow—he's written a treatise, an article or something, and wants it polished up a bit. I mentioned your name. He's not particularly bright, poor fellow. It's probably all a lot of drivel, but when you see him just flatter him a bit.

GLOUMOV, *in a shocked voice.* Oh, Uncle! You're asking me to do a thing like that!

MAMAEV. I'm not suggesting one should flatter people all the time, but there's no harm in just buttering him up a bit. Just one or two compliments on his style or something will give pleasure to the poor old fellow. He can be useful to you at the moment. Later on, we can abuse him as much as we like, but not for the moment. He's gone now, but I'll take you to see him tomorrow. Then there's another rather delicate matter. . . . What exactly are your relations with your aunt?

GLOUMOV. I beg your pardon, Uncle?

MAMAEV. How are you behaving to her?

GLOUMOV. Correctly, I hope, Uncle.

MAMAEV. Never mind correctness! If you don't understand what I'm driving at, you must listen and learn. And be grateful you have someone to teach you! Women aren't interested in correctness of behaviour. All they want is their beauty to be recognised.

GLOUMOV. Oh yes, yes, uncle, of course, how stupid of me! It simply never entered my head!

MAMAEV. Well, there you are, my boy. I know of course you're really only a second cousin of ours, or something, but still you are related. You can be much freer with my wife than if you were just a mere acquaintance; there's no reason why you shouldn't sometimes, say . . . absentmindedly kiss her hand—then having kissed it once, kiss it again, or . . . do something with your eyes. I suppose you know how to do it?

GLOUMOV. I'm afraid I don't.

MAMAEV. Good heavens, you've a lot to learn! Well, like this. *Rolls up his eyes.*

GLOUMOV. Don't, don't, Uncle. What on earth are you doing?

MAMAEV. You just practise it properly in front of a mirror. Then you must sigh sometimes. That always goes down very well with them.

GLOUMOV. What sort of sigh should I give, Uncle?

MAMAEV. You know the sort of thing. Very languid, as if you couldn't stand it any longer. Like this.
Heaves deep sigh.
But it needs practice, mind. You must practise it.

GLOUMOV. I will, indeed, I will, uncle, and thank you very, very much for your advice.

MAMAEV. Not at all, my boy. I feel much easier in my mind now I've spoken to you. Do you understand?

GLOUMOV. No—I'm afraid I don't.

MAMAEV. Bless the boy! Well, she's a woman of very—ah—passionate temperament. She gets very easily heated. It's quite on the cards that she might become infatuated with some young scoundrel, one of these dandies, you know the sort of type. You never can tell, she might even fall in love with an escaped convict. Whereas here you are, a decent young fellow, one that I can heartily approve of—in the words of the old proverb: the wolf will be satisfied and the sheep will remain untouched.
Laughs loudly.
Now do you understand?

GLOUMOV. I can hardly speak, uncle.

MAMAEV. Hardly speak, why?

GLOUMOV. It takes my breath away, the amazing power of your brain!

MAMAEV. Well, it's always at your service, my boy, as long as you come to me for advice.

GLOUMOV. Uncle . . . I've had an idea. I don't suppose it's much good but——

MAMAEV. Come on, let's hear it.

GLOUMOV. Well, you know how careful one has to be in Moscow society—there's so much whispering and scandalmongering. Now suppose you were to introduce me to Madame Tourousina, for instance, I could openly pay court to her niece and even propose to her if you approved. All eyes would be fixed on that and no one would notice what Aunt Kleopatra and I were doing. Then indeed the wolves really would be satisfied and the sheep remain untouched.

MAMAEV. Good, my boy, good! A very sound idea.

GLOUMOV. Of course, it wouldn't do to let Auntie know anything about it. Not that she'd be jealous but—it's always best to use a little tact with women.

MAMAEV. Don't I know it! We won't say a word to her then—not a word!

GLOUMOV. Er—when did you say you were taking me to Madame Tourousina's, Uncle?

MAMAEV. Any time you like. Tomorrow evening? And don't forget to do everything I've told you. As soon as we get there, start on the niece.

KLEOPATRA, *entering from the ballroom, followed by* GORODOULIN. No, no, no, not tonight. I'm grateful for your help, Ivan, but not tonight.
To MAMAEV.
Ivan's going now.

MAMAEV. So early?
Shaking hands with him.
Well, glad you could come.

GORODOULIN. It's been enchanting.
To GLOUMOV.
Goodby. Let me know when you've completed that little matter we spoke of.

GLOUMOV. I shall send it to you in the morning.

MAMAEV. Er—Gorodoulin, I want a word with you in connection with the club. I want to give you some advice.

GORODOULIN, *hastily*. I—I haven't time, if you'll excuse me.
Looking at his watch.
I'm in a great hurry, I really haven't a minute. Goodnight, Kleopatra.
Kisses her hand. To GLOUMOV.
Au revoir.

MAMAEV, *following him out*. That's all right, I'll walk part of the way with you. I can give you some advice on the way.

KLEOPATRA, *sinking into a chair*. Well, I've settled it.
She holds out her hand for him to kiss.
A job for you. And a very good one too, in the Civil Service.

GLOUMOV. Oh, Kleopatra!
Kisses her hand.
Why did you do it? I'd never have asked you to do a thing like this for me.

KLEOPATRA. You'd no need to. I guessed.

GLOUMOV, *impulsively, kissing her hand again*. Thank you! Thank you!
Suddenly he dashes off in the direction of the ballroom.

KLEOPATRA, *sharply*. Where are you going?

GLOUMOV. To find Mamma. I'm so happy. I must share my happiness with her.

KLEOPATRA. Are you sure you're happy, Yegor?

GLOUMOV. As happy as I can ever hope to be.

KLEOPATRA. Do you mean—there's something lacking to make your happiness complete?

GLOUMOV, *after a pause*. There's nothing more I dare hope for.

KLEOPATRA. Now come, be frank with me. What do you want more than anything in the world?

GLOUMOV. I've a job in the Civil Service. What more could a man ask?

KLEOPATRA. I don't believe it—not for a moment! You expect me to believe that you, Yegor, with your eyes, your brow—are a common materialist who wants nothing more from life than a weekly salary and a job in the Civil Service.

GLOUMOV. Kleopatra! . . .

KLEOPATRA. You expect me to believe that your heart never beats, that you never dream, never cry, never lie awake at nights, that you love no one?

GLOUMOV. No, no, Kleopatra, I didn't say that.

KLEOPATRA. Then you do love someone?
He hangs his head.
I knew it, I knew it, and she doesn't love you in return. Who is she, tell me, who is this cruel woman?

GLOUMOV. Oh my God, Kleopatra, this is agony!

KLEOPATRA. Tell me, tell me, Yegor, I insist. I know it all, I can see it in your eyes. Poor darling boy, are you suffering very much?

GLOUMOV. Don't, I can't bear it! In a minute I shall have to tell you! It's not fair to try and trick me like this.

KLEOPATRA. Who is she, who is it you love?

GLOUMOV. Have pity on me, for the love of heaven!

KLEOPATRA. Is she worthy of you?

GLOUMOV. Oh, my God, what are you doing to me!

KLEOPATRA. Is she capable of responding to your passion? Could she understand your noble suffering heart?

GLOUMOV. Kill me, kill me with your own hands, Kleopatra, but I dare not tell you!

KLEOPATRA, *faintly.* Whisper, only whisper the name.

GLOUMOV. The name of the woman I love?

KLEOPATRA. Yes. . . .

GLOUMOV, *falling on his knees.* You.

KLEOPATRA. Ah. . . .

GLOUMOV. Beat me, kill me, punish me in any way you will, only don't send me away from you! Force me to be silent, forbid me even to look at you any more, tell me I'm to be cold and distant to you, but don't, don't I beg of you, be angry with me! It's all your own fault! Why were you so kind, so enchanting, so gracious to me? If you'd been harsh and cruel, then I might have kept my passion within the bounds of decency! But you heavenly adorable woman, angel of goodness that you are, you've turned me, a sane, reasonable man, into a crazy madman!

Springing to his feet.

Yes, I am mad! I'm not responsible for my actions any more. One moment longer with you and I don't know what I might do! . . . Oh my God, what have I said? Forgive me, forgive me.

Flinging himself on his knees again and trying to kiss the hem of her garment.

KLEOPATRA. I forgive you, Yegor.

Springing up again he clasps her in his arms. They kiss. He gives her a wild look and dashes back to the ballroom. The band strikes up a furious gallop, and KLEOPATRA *sinks on to a chair in a swoon of delight.*

Curtain

ACT TWO

SCENE 1

The drawing-room of a country house a few miles outside Moscow. Two elderly women, MADAME TOUROUSINA's *"companions," are enjoying a siesta.* MATRIOSHA, *round and plump, warms herself before the stove, her skirts pulled over her knees.* LUBINKA, *an untidy, witch-like creature, nods over a bottle of vodka and some playing cards. At the sound of raised voices in the passage, both open their eyes with a start and busy themselves,* MATRIOSHA—*after pulling her skirts down—with some sewing snatched up from the floor,* LUBINKA, *hastily concealing the vodka bottle, with laying out the cards.*

MADAME T., *off.* No, no! I won't set foot outside the house again today!

MATRIOSHA *and* LUBINKA *exchange glances.*

MASHENKA, *off.* Oh, Auntie, *please,* Auntie!

MADAME TOUROUSINA, *a woman in her late forties, still beautiful in spite of her unhealthy pallor, enters, followed by her niece,* MASHENKA.

MADAME T. Not for anything in the world. It would be sheer madness. Besides I've had the horses unharnessed.

Sinking into a chair, a hand to her brow.

Oh, I'm quite exhausted. Matriosha—the footstool.

MATRIOSHA *heaves herself up and brings the stool over.*

MATRIOSHA. Aren't you going for your drive, dear?

LUBINKA, *coming down from card table.* I told you she'd be ill today. I saw it in the cards.

MATRIOSHA. Yes, she told me.

MASHENKA. Auntie's not ill. What *is* the matter, auntie darling? It's the first time for months we've been for a drive, we hardly get ten yards from the gates and we have to turn back again!

Flinging herself disconsolately into a chair.

MADAME T. Why run into danger when it's not necessary?

MASHENKA. But what danger? I didn't see any.

MADAME T. I really wonder sometimes, darling, whether you're quite right in the head. You must have seen that white cat cross the path in front of us as we came out of the gates.

MATRIOSHA, *in a tone of alarm.* It crossed the path in front of you?

LUBINKA. From the right or the left, was it?

MADAME T., *dramatically.* From the *left.*

LUBINKA
MATRIOSHA } *gasping and shaking their heads.* Tch, tch, tch.

MATRIOSHA. You poor dear. It must have given you a shock.

MADAME T. I wanted to give orders to stop but I thought, no, no, I must be brave, it's no good giving in.
Gasps of admiration from the companions.

LUBINKA. She's always the same. She will carry on whatever happens.

MATRIOSHA. Never thinks of herself. She must be more careful.

MADAME T. It was Mashenka I was thinking of. My heart was right up in my throat. But I wouldn't say anything, so we drove on and we hadn't gone more than a few yards when suddenly I saw, coming down the road towards us, a man in a brown hat.
MATRIOSHA *and* LUBINKA *draw in their breaths with horror.*

MASHENKA, *dryly.* On the left or the right side of the road?

MADAME T. I've told you before, I will not have you making fun of these things.

MASHENKA. Well, as if it could make any difference!

MADAME T. You know quite well it's a sign of terrible misfortune. I will not have this free-thinking in my house, Mashenka. You can go to your room if you persist. There's quite enough blasphemy from the guests who come here. I have to put up with that, but I will not put up with it from you.
While she is talking the two companions move back to their seats and resume their occupations.
Surely, Mashenka, it's our duty to preserve our lives. What's the purpose of signs and warnings if we're merely to ignore them. Look at the dreadful accidents one hears about nowadays. The horses bolt, the carriage overturns, the coachman gets drunk and lands in a ditch! If God takes the trouble to send us a sign—two signs in fact—telling us not to go out today, the least we can do is to take notice of them.

MASHENKA. But God didn't tell us not to go out today.

MADAME T., *wearily closing her eyes.* Please darling, this dreadful free-thinking in a child of your age. . . . If there were a vital necessity to go out it would be a different matter, but to risk one's life merely to spend an evening in empty conversation, or discussing one's neighbours! No, I don't think so! ...

Pulling herself together.

Matriosha and Lubinka, go into the morning room.

MATRIOSHA *takes up her sewing*, LUBINKA *her cards and they hurry out. Turning to her niece*, MADAME TOUROUSINA *addresses her in more practical tones.*

I know quite well why you're so keen on going there today. You're hoping to meet Yegor Kourchaev who's nothing but an atheist and whom I will not allow to enter my house. And so you try to drag your aunt there, not giving a thought to the fact that I may break an arm or a leg just so that you can enjoy yourself.

MASHENKA. I don't understand why you dislike Yegor so much.

MADAME T. Because he laughs at the most sacred things in my presence.

MASHENKA. But when, Auntie, when?

MADAME T. Continually. He's always laughing at the holy pilgrims who come here. He even laughs at my having poor Lubinka and Matriosha as companions.

MASHENKA. But you said he laughed at sacred things.

MADAME T. Well, of course he does. Only the other day I was saying, "Look, my Matriosha's face is beginning to shine with saintliness," and do you know what he dared to say to me? "It's not with saintliness," he said, "its with grease." And I won't forgive that sort of remark. That's what free-thinking leads to! No, I seldom make a mistake in people and you see what sort of man he's turned out to be. I got two more of those letters about him yesterday. You can read them if you like.

MASHENKA. I know auntie, but surely you don't take any notice of anonymous letters?

MADAME T. If there'd only been one I might not, but several! ... And from different people.

GRIGORI, *the servant, comes in with a letter which he hands to her.*

GRIGORI, *sourly.* Those tramps are downstairs again.

MADAME T. Tramps? I don't know whom you're referring to. You don't mean my holy pilgrims, do you?

GRIGORI. Tramps I call them, madam.

MADAME T. That's quite enough, Grigori. You know my orders. Any pilgrims that come to my house are to be taken to the kitchen and given a good meal.

GRIGORI goes out. MADAME TOUROUSINA *opens the letter.*

Here you are, here's another one! Obviously written by a most trustworthy woman.

Reads aloud.

"Dear Madam, though I have not the pleasure of . . ."

Reads to herself.

Here you are, listen! "I am filled with horror at your choice of a creature like Yegor Kourchaev and I tremble to think of what will happen to poor Mashenka. Do you realise that he is a well-known liberal . . ." and so on and so on.

MASHENKA. May I see?

Taking the letter and looking at it.

Isn't it extraordinary? I just don't know what to think about it.

MADAME T. Well, Mashenka dear, if you persist in going your own way I shall do nothing to stop you.

Sniffing at her smelling salts.

Nobody shall say I've treated you like a tyrant, but you know what very deep distress you're causing me and you can hardly complain if I . . .

MASHENKA. Don't give me a dowry?

MADAME T. And more important still, dear, my blessing!

MASHENKA. Oh, don't worry, Auntie. I wouldn't dream of marrying without a dowry. I like Yegor Kourchaev very much, but if you won't give me one there's no more to be said. I shan't pine away or go into a decline. But, Auntie darling, try to understand what I feel. I'm quite well off, thanks to you, but I want to enjoy myself, to get something out of life.

MADAME T. I know, I know, dear.

MASHENKA. I'll marry anybody you find for me, as long as he's not too boring. I want to go about in society. After all, I'm quite pretty, I want to be admired. But the tedium of living as we do, Auntie! It's too much, you must admit.

MADAME T. Oh well, one can't be cross with you at your age.

MASHENKA. I've no doubt I shall live exactly your sort of life when I'm older. It's in the family.

MADAME T. I only pray that you do, darling. I pray with all my soul! It's the right road, the straight road.

MASHENKA. I know, Auntie. But I must have a gay time first. Please, can't you arrange a marriage for me?

MADAME T. It's so difficult nowadays. The young men are so spoiled.

MASHENKA. Oh dear! Surely there must be someone in Moscow! Couldn't you ask some of your friends, Mr. Kroutitzky, for instance, Mr. Mamaev, or Mr. Gorodoulin? They'd be delighted to help you find a husband for me.

MADAME T., *with a tired laugh.* They're only human beings. They can be misled and they can mislead other people.

MASHENKA. Well then, what are we to do?

MADAME T. We must wait for a sign. I shan't make any decision until we receive some special sign.

MASHENKA. And where's this sign to come from?

MADAME T. You'll know soon enough when the time comes; today perhaps.

MASHENKA. Auntie, don't forbid him the house. Do let him come here.

MADAME T. Who?

MASHENKA. Yegor Kourchaev.

MADAME T. As long as you realise he's not the man for you.

MASHENKA. Whatever you say, auntie. I'm your obedient, dutiful little niece.

MADAME T., *kissing her.* You're a dear child.

MASHENKA. I'm determined to be rich and lead a gay life. Auntie, you used to lead a gay life, usen't you?

MADAME T. I—I can't remember.

MASHENKA. Oh, auntie, you did! A very, very gay life.

MADAME T. Oh—you know quite a lot, I see. But whatever you know, dear, I'd much rather you didn't know any more.

MASHENKA. I think you're the very best woman in the world, and I'm going to base my life on yours. I shall have the gayest of gay times and then repent. Sin and repent, just like you.

MADAME T. I don't know what you're talking about, Mashenka!

GRIGORI, *entering.* Mr. Kroutitzky, madam.

MADAME T. Show him in.
Sniffing her smelling salts.
My head's aching with all your prattle, Mashenka dear. Go and amuse yourself in the garden or the library, I'll see Mr. Kroutitzky alone.

MASHENKA, *going towards the garden.* All right, Auntie. Don't forget to ask him, will you?

MADAME T. Ask him what?

MASHENKA. If he knows of a young man for me.

MADAME T. All right, my pet. Run away, run away.

GRIGORI, *entering.* Mr. Kroutitzky.
MASHENKA runs out. KROUTITZKY, enters and GRIGORI goes out.

MADAME T., *smiling wanly at him.* What a pleasant surprise!

KROUTITZKY, *taking her hand.* You're very pale, my dear. Nerves bad again?

MADAME T. My nerves are in a dreadful state.

KROUTITZKY. Your hands are cold, too. I wish you'd give up all this——

MADAME T., *defensively*. Give up what?

KROUTITZKY. Too much religion's bad for the nerves.

MADAME T. I've told you before. I won't discuss it with you.

KROUTITZKY. I'm only saying that in the old days when you
   went about and enjoyed yourself you were a different
   woman. Why, I remember one night when——

MADAME T. Oh don't, don't remind me of it!

KROUTITZKY. Why not? There was a great deal that was very
   good in your old life and if there happened to have been
   a few things that you'd—er—rather not think about now,
   well I'm sure you've amply atoned for them. Personally, I
   look back on some of them with a great deal of pleasure.
   Far from repenting, I like to recall every detail and enjoy
   them again.
   Chuckling reminiscently.
   Do you remember that occasion when we——

MADAME T. Stop! Stop!
   As GRIGORI enters.
   Yes, what is it, Grigori?

GRIGORI. That dirty old tramp's downstairs again.

MADAME T. How dare you refer to a holy pilgrim like that?
   You should be ashamed of yourself! Take him to the kitchen
   and see that he's given a good meal.
   GRIGORI *goes, muttering under his breath.*
   The ignorance of these servants!

KROUTITZKY. Well, to return to what I was saying, when you
   lived a different kind of life you were much healthier.

MADAME T. Physically I may have been, not spiritually.

KROUTITZKY. At any rate you looked healthier then. But you're
   still young. You've plenty of time to enjoy yourself.

MADAME T. I've no desire for that sort of enjoyment.

KROUTITZKY. If I were you I should postpone repenting till
   your looks start to go.

MADAME T. I've already asked you not to——

KROUTITZKY. Sorry, sorry, I won't.

GRIGORI, *entering.* There's another of those dirty tramps come now.

MADAME T. I've told you once already. You're not to refer to them like that. Take him into the kitchen with the others. See that he's given a good meal.

GRIGORI. I won't go into the kitchen, madam, not with them there. I can't stand the stench.

MADAME T. Do as I tell you at once!

GRIGORI *goes out, grumbling under his breath.*

KROUTITZKY. You ought to be more careful whom you ask into your house.

MADAME T. I'm quite capable of looking after myself.

KROUTITZKY. Well, be careful, my dear, that's all. It's a well-known fact that a woman who takes up religion is fair game for all kinds of charlatans and swindlers. It's very easy to make a fool of her.

MADAME T. Do you think I wouldn't know if someone were trying to deceive me? Do you think God wouldn't send some sign? Why, only today I was saved from the most dreadful accident. If it hadn't been for God warning me not to go out, the carriage would have overturned and I should be lying in the road, a mangled corpse with broken arms and legs.

KROUTITZKY. Well, as you didn't go out, how do you know the carriage would have overturned?

MADAME T., *with an exasperated sigh.* There are some things one can't discuss with you. Let's not talk of it. . . . Will you give me your advice on a very important matter?

KROUTITZKY. With pleasure. I'm always delighted to be of service to you. What is it?

Moving closer to her.

MADAME T., *moving away from him.* You know Mashenka's reached the age when she——

KROUTITZKY. Yes, yes, I know.

MADAME T. Do you know of a young man for her?

KROUTITZKY. None whom you'd approve of, I'm afraid.

MADAME T. *with a sigh*. That's the trouble.
A pause.

KROUTITZKY. Wait a minute! . . . I know exactly the right young fellow for you.

MADAME T. Really?

KROUTITZKY. Yes. He's extremely charming, rather shy and diffident, has the right ideas and comes of a good family. He was recommended to me for a small job I wanted done, so I put him through his paces and I can tell you he's a most exceptional fellow.

MADAME T. But who is he?

KROUTITZKY. What's his name? Oh lord, what a memory! Wait a minute though, he gave me his address.
Takes out some papers from his pocket and goes through them.
Ah, here it is! Yegor Dimitrich Gloumov. A very beautiful hand, too: even lettering—that means he's methodical, no flourishes—that means he's not a free-thinker. . . . Here, keep it. It may be useful to you.

MADAME T., *taking it*. Thank you.

KROUTITZKY. Well, I hope it comes to something. One likes to help on the young people.
Looking at his watch.
I must be getting along.
Taking the hand which she extends to him.
Good-bye, Sophia. May I come again or are you angry with me?

MADAME T. You know I'm always glad to see you.

KROUTITZKY. If I weren't fond of you I wouldn't speak so frankly.

MADAME T., Do come again.

KROUTITZKY. For old time's sake?

Laughs knowingly. MADAME TOUROUSINA *closes her eyes, wrinkling her brow with displeasure.*

Well, I'd better go before you're cross with me again. . . . Au revoir.

He goes out.

MADAME T., *to herself.* At his age too! . . .

She takes out the piece of paper and studies it. MASHENKA *appears from the garden.*

MASHENKA. Has he gone?

MADAME T. Mashenka, you've not been eavesdropping?

MASHENKA, *coming into the room.* Of course not, Auntie. Did he think of anyone for me?

GRIGORI, *entering.* Mr. Gorodoulin, madam.

MADAME T. Show him in.

MASHENKA. I'm sure *he'll* know of someone. Don't forget to ask, will you? Anybody you like, but he mustn't be too tedious.

She runs out.

GRIGORI, *appearing at the door again.* Mr. Gorodoulin.
GORODOULIN *comes in and* GRIGORI *goes out.*

MADAME T. Well, aren't you ashamed of yourself? Where have you been hiding all these weeks?

GORODOULIN. I haven't had a moment. Business appointments, official dinners, then there was the opening of the railway.

MADAME T. I don't believe a word of it. I think you just find it dull here. . . . Anyway, it's nice of you to call and see me sometimes. Sit down. . . . I've been hoping for some news from you.

GORODOULIN. News? Of what?

MADAME T. You don't mean to tell me you've forgotten! Well, that's charming, that's very kind of you. I'm sorry, I should have realised that a person who has such important matters to attend to, could hardly find time to worry about the poor and oppressed. Such trivialities are beneath your notice, of course.

GORODOULIN. This is the first I've heard about the poor and oppressed. I remember you asked me to make some enquiries about some fortuneteller.

MADAME T. Nothing of the sort! A clairvoyante! There's a great difference. I would never have gone to a fortuneteller.

GORODOULIN. Sorry. I confess my ignorance of these subtle distinctions. Well, anyway, it was about Oulita Schmigaeva, widow of an old clothes dealer.

MADAME T. Her social status has nothing to do with it. She's a most remarkable woman and I'm proud, yes proud, that she's granted her special favors to me.

GORODOULIN. She's granted most of those to a discharged sailor.

MADAME T. That's the most disgusting slander! Why, she's been received in the best houses in Moscow. It's envy, it's jealousy, that's all it is, because she's been successful. Oh—the world's too evil to live in! . . . But she'll be acquitted. You'll see, God will vindicate her.

GORODOULIN. I'm afraid she'll have to tell fortunes in Siberia now.

MADAME T., *springing to her feet.* So that's your famous court of justice! To send an innocent woman to Siberia! For what? For doing good to others!

GORODOULIN. But she's been convicted of fortunetelling.

MADAME T. I'll tell you what it is. It's all part of a plot to turn us into atheists. Oh, yes, you can laugh at me but mark my words, she was convicted because she was believed! As *I* would be convicted if some people had their way.

GORODOULIN. Quite apart from fortunetelling, she was accused of receiving stolen goods, keeping a brothel and poisoning a commercial traveller.

MADAME T. I don't believe a word of it! Who—who said so?

GORODOULIN. It's the solemn truth. The commercial traveller's wife went to her to have her fortune told and came away with a recipe that was guaranteed to reawaken her husband's passion. Well, she brewed this concoction according to the instructions and gave it to him in a glass of port. But she'd forgotten one thing—to ask permission of the Ministry of Health.

MADAME T. What happened to the commercial traveller?

GORODOULIN. It worked. He died. But not from love.

MADAME T. I suppose you find that funny. There were plenty of people to plot against this poor woman it seems, but no one to defend her.

GORODOULIN. Not at all. She had the best lawyer in Moscow. A positive torrent of eloquence flowed through the court, overflowed the banks and finally quieted down to a scarcely audible whisper. All to no purpose—because she confessed —after the discharged sailor had given her away.

MADAME T. I'd never have believed it! . . . It only shows how easily one can be mistaken in people. It's impossible to live in this world.

GORODOULIN. It's not impossible, but it's difficult unless one can see it clearly as it is. There've been great strides in the studies of mental diseases and hallucinations lately and——

MADAME T. I've told you before I don't want to discuss the subject.

GORODOULIN. Sorry. I forgot.

MADAME T. Let me be mistaken in people, let me be deceived. My only happiness is in helping the poor and oppressed.

GRIGORI, *entering.* There's *another* dirty old tramp downstairs.

GORODOULIN. What, another?

MADAME T. I don't understand what you're referring to.

GRIGORI. Sorry, madam, a holy pilgrim.

MADAME T. That's better. What is he like?

GRIGORI. Well, he scared me. He gave me a terrible turn. It gives you a turn just to look at him even.

MADAME T. What do you mean "gives you a turn"? What nonsense!

GRIGORI. He's so fierce-looking, madam. All covered in hair. You can only see his eyes.

MADAME T. He must be an Italian.

ACT TWO *Scene 1* 59

GRIGORI. No, I don't think he's an Italian, madam. He's not quite the right color. If you ask me he's a proper Hungarian.

MADAME T. A Hungarian?

GRIGORI. That's it, madam. The kind that sells mousetraps.

MADAME T. Well, take him into the kitchen, see that he gets a good meal and ask him if there's anything he needs.

GRIGORI. They're getting very noisy in there, madam. One of them's got a bottle of——

MADAME T. Don't talk so much, Grigori. Do as I say at once.

GRIGORI. Yes, madam.

He goes.

MADAME T., *seeing the smirk on* GORODOULIN's *face.* Spare me your humorous comments, Ivan. . . . Listen, I want to ask you something. It's about Mashenka. Do you know of a nice young man for her?

GORODOULIN. I hardly think I'm the right person to come to. You can't say that I look like a matchmaker. I'm against any form of chains, even matrimonial ones.

MADAME T. But you wear them yourself.

GORODOULIN. That's why I wouldn't condemn my worst enemy to wear them.

MADAME T. Seriously though, can you think of anyone?

GORODOULIN. Wait a minute! I did meet someone the other day who had "ideal husband" written in large letters across his forehead.

MADAME T. Who was it? Do try and remember.

GORODOULIN. Oh yes . . . Gloumov.

MADAME T. Is he a *good* young man?

GORODOULIN. He's thoroughly trustworthy, I'm sure. I think he's a very nice fellow.

MADAME T. Wait a minute. What did you say his name was? *Taking out the paper which* KROUTITZKY *gave her.*

GORODOULIN. Gloumov.

MADAME T. Yegor Dimitrich?

GORODOULIN. Yes.

MADAME T. How extraordinary. Anton Kroutitzky only mentioned him to me just now.

GORODOULIN. Well, that must mean he's the right man. He can't escape his fate. Or perhaps destiny would be more tactful. . . . I must go.

MADAME T. Well, good-bye. I won't keep you from all your important appointments.

GORODOULIN. Let me know if my matchmaking proves successful.

MADAME T. I will, of course. And thank you for the advice. Good-bye.

He goes out. MADAME TOUROUSINA *rises and begins to pace the room, glancing occasionally at the paper in her hand.*

MADAME T. Yegor Gloumov. . . . Yegor Gloumov. . . .

Going to the door, she calls.

Matriosha, Lubinka.

After a second or two they come in, LUBINKA *holding her pack of cards,* MATRIOSHA *carrying a small poodle in her arms.* MADAME TOUROUSINA *sinks into the chair again.* I don't know what to think. Both Mr. Kroutitzky and Mr. Gorodoulin have suggested the same young man for Mashenka but I haven't confidence in either of them. Still, there must be something in it if they both think highly of him. Oh . . . what a loss for Moscow when Ivan Yakovlevitch died. He was the last of the Russian saints in my opinion. Life was so easy, so simple, when he was here. I can't sleep at night now for wondering what I'm going to do with Mashenka; and if I make a mistake, the sin will be on my own head. If he were alive still, I'd have nothing to think about even. I'd go and ask him what to do and there'd be nothing more to worry about. I wonder if this Madame Maniefa will take his place? I think there's something very supernatural about her, don't you?

MATRIOSHA, *bringing the footstool.* Oh, yes. They say Peter the Great appeared to her in a cloud and she just gave one look at a lady with toothache and the tooth stopped aching.

MADAME T. Don't drop the poodle, Matriosha.

LUBINKA, *who has seated herself at the table*. Shall I lay the cards out?

MADAME T. In a minute.

The sound of wild music accompanied by shouts and cries, which for the last few minutes has been increasing in volume, is now loud enough to force itself on MADAME TOUROUSINA'S *attention.*

Listen, what's that? It sounds like gypsies.

LUBINKA. It's those pilgrims, dear.

MASHENKA, *running in from the garden*. Auntie, those pilgrims are having a party in the yard. Varya and Masha and the new cook are all dancing with them.

MADAME T. Oh, the world's too evil for me. . . .

MASHENKA. May I go and watch?

MADAME T. No, no, Mashenka, stay here. I want to talk to you.

MASHENKA. What did Mr. Gorodoulin say?

MADAME T. Well, it's very strange but he and Mr. Kroutitzky both suggested the same young man.

MASHENKA. Auntie, how wonderful! He's bound to be nice then.

MADAME T. Well, I don't entirely trust them.

LUBINKA. Shall I start, dear?

MADAME T. Yes, tell my fortune. See if they spoke the truth. *To* MASHENKA.

No, I don't trust them. They could easily be mistaken.

MASHENKA. But why, Auntie darling?

MADAME T. Because they're ordinary human beings.

MASHENKA, *disconsolately*. Who will you ever believe then? Nothing will ever get settled. It quite frightens me.

MADAME T. Of course it does, darling. You *should* feel frightened. How can we raise even a corner of the veil which hides our future without feeling afraid? Behind that veil lie your happiness, your unhappiness, your life and your death. Matriosha, don't drop the poodle.

MASHENKA. But who's going to raise it for us?

MADAME T. There is someone in Moscow, darling. One living being who has the power.

GRIGORI, *entering.* There's a person to see you, madam.

MADAME T. *eagerly.* Who is it?

GRIGORI. She says her name's Madame Maniefa.

MADAME T., *getting to her feet.* Show her in at once. It's she, it's she, Mashenka.

To the two companions who have also got to their feet. How extraordinary her coming just at this moment, as if she knew what was happening, could read our thoughts! . . .

MADAME MANIEFA *appears at the door. As usual, she is slightly drunk.*

Come in, please come in, we didn't expect such an honour. Matriosha, Lubinka, lead Madame Maniefa to a chair. Never mind the poodle.

They hurry to support her on either side. The barbaric music from the yard adds to the impression that a ritual is taking place.

MANIEFA. There's holiness in the house when she who's holy brings her holiness to the holy ones.

MATRIOSHA. O, did you hear that, Lubinka?

MADAME T. Be quiet, can't you. Mashenka, take that dog outside.

MASHENKA *does so.*

MANIEFA, *as she is lowered into the chair.* She came like a bird and went like another bird.

LUBINKA. Oh Matriosha, did you hear that?

MATRIOSHA. Isn't she wonderful?

To MADAME TOUROUSINA.

Did you hear that, dear?

MANIEFA, *suddenly.* Who do you think you're staring at?

MADAME T. We're all so happy that you've come to visit us. God grant we're not too unworthy.

MATRIOSHA. Yes, God grant we're not!

LUBINKA, *to* MADAME TOUROUSINA. *You're* not, dear.
To MADAME MANIEFA.
She's a saint if ever there was one.

MADAME T., *to* MANIEFA. May we humbly ask you to speak to us? Have you a message for us?
MADAME MANIEFA *appears to go into a trance.*

LUBINKA. Oh, my God, it's the spirits descending into her.

MATRIOSHA. Oh, my holy fathers!

MADAME T. Ssh, listen! Support her, hold her hands. If she gets a shock she might die.
They do so.

MANIEFA, *in a voice like a little girl.* They expected her in slippers and she came in boots.

LUBINKA, *in a hoarse whisper.* Remember that, don't forget what she said! . . .

MADAME T. Memorise it somebody! Ssh, she's going to speak again.
Nothing happens. MADAME TOUROUSINA *ventures in an awestruck voice.*
I wanted to ask you. . . .

MANIEFA. The one who knows runs, the one who doesn't lies down. One girl less—one woman more.

MATRIOSHA. Oh, my God, isn't it wonderful!

LUBINKA. It's a spirit speaking! . . .
Whispering to MADAME TOUROUSINA.
Ask her who it is, dear!

MADAME T. No, no, no! Do stop.
Then humbly to MADAME MANIEFA.
Have you something to tell us about a young man? Won't

you say something to your servant Sophia? Don't you see a young man in your vision?

MANIEFA. I see a cloud, the cloud is shifting. In the centre of the cloud is Yegor.

MATRIOSHA. Yegor!

LUBINKA. Did you hear that, dear?

MASHENKA, *whispering in her aunt's ear.* But, Auntie, that's Mr. Kourchaev's name.

MADAME T. Ssh. . . . May we humbly ask, who is Yegor?

MANIEFA. When you see, you'll know.

MADAME T. When shall we see him?

MANIEFA. A guest who is wanted, need not be invited.

LUBINKA, *in a whisper to* MADAME TOUROUSINA. There you are, dear.

MADAME T. Please tell us, how can we recognise him?

MATRIOSHA, *To* MADAME TOUROUSINA *in a whisper.* Ask what colour his hair is!

MADAME T. Oh, be quiet.
Then resuming her humble, awestruck tone.
Is he dark or fair?

MANIEFA. To some he is dark, to you he is fair.

MASHENKA, *in a whisper.* Mr. Kourchaev's fair, auntie.

MADAME T. Don't be so silly. As if a Hussar could appear in a vision.

LUBINKA. It's wonderful, even the cards said Yegor.

MADAME T. What are you talking about? How can you see a name in the cards?

LUBINKA. I'm sorry, dear. I didn't mean that. I meant I saw a fair man in the cards.

MADAME T. Ssh, she's going to speak again.

MANIEFA. The stranger is far away but the one who is coming is at the gate.

MADAME T. ⎫
MATRIOSHA. ⎬ At the gate?
MASHENKA. ⎭

MANIEFA. Get ready, prepare the banquet, visitors are coming.

MADAME T. When? When?

MATRIOSHA. ⎫ When?
LUBINKA. ⎭

MANIEFA. Now . . . they are here.
Her head falls forward.

GRIGORI, *entering.* Mr. Mamaev to see you, madam.
All except MADAME MANIEFA, *turn and look at him.*

MADAME T. Alone?

GRIGORI. There's a young gentleman with him, madam.

MADAME T. A—fair young gentleman?

GRIGORI. That's right, madam.

LUBINKA. Oh, isn't it wonderful!

MATRIOSHA. I can't believe it! It's like a dream!

MADAME T., *flinging her arms round* MASHENKA. Mashenka, darling, my prayers have been answered.

MASHENKA. It's all so peculiar, Auntie. I—I'm trembling all over.
MADAME MANIEFA, *forgotten for the moment, draws attention to herself by a groan.* MADAME TOUROUSINA *flies to her.*

MADAME T. Madame Maniefa, are you all right?

MANIEFA. Where am I?

MADAME T. You're amongst friends. You've had a vision.

MANIEFA. I'll be all right when I've had a drop of something.

MADAME T. Lead her into the dining-room and give her tea, tea.

MANIEFA. Tea's no good after a vision.

MADAME T., *as they start to lead her off.* Vodka, then, wine, anything.

LUBINKA. Wait, wait, we must have a glimpse of him, just one glimpse.

MATRIOSHA. It's a miracle, that's what it is, dear, a miracle!
MAMAEV and GLOUMOV appear at the door.

MAMAEV. Sophia Ignatieva—allow me to present my nephew, Yegor Dimitrich Gloumov.

LUBINKA. Exactly as she described!

MATRIOSHA. Fair hair and all!

MAMAEV. He's a good lad, you'll like him.

MADAME T., *holding out her hand for GLOUMOV to kiss.* I shall love him as my own son.

   Curtain

ACT TWO

SCENE 2

The same as Act One, Scene 1. STYOPKA *as usual, is lolling in his shirtsleeves, picking his teeth.*

GLOUMOV, *calling through the door to his mother's bedroom.* Mamma, aren't you going to Madame Tourousina's?

MADAME G. *off.* All right, I'm coming. What's the hurry?

GLOUMOV. You're late!
Coming back into the room followed by his mother who is putting on her bonnet.
You should be there first thing in the morning, every day. You ought practically to live there.

MADAME G. I can't do more. I do my best. I'm worn out with it.
Giving STYOPKA *a push.*

For the love of God, go out and do the shopping. Nothing to eat in the house as usual. The whole place'll go to rack and ruin with me out all day!

GLOUMOV *has seated himself at the table and is writing in his diary.*

What are you putting in that diary now?

GLOUMOV. Another stupid conversation with Mr. Kroutitzky. Heaven knows how I remember it all.

MADAME G. Heaven knows what Kleopatra's going to say when she finds out you're engaged. *Has* she found out?

GLOUMOV. I don't know. I wish I did, then I'd know how to handle her.

MADAME G. Yes, it's very worrying.

STYOPKA, *who has been moving lazily about the room, pulling on his jacket.* We don't want her upsetting everything just when you're getting us on our feet.

MADAME G., *to* STYOPKA. You get on your feet down to Smirnoff's and get some provisions in.

To herself.

Lazy dolt!

STYOPKA, *ignoring her and talking to* GLOUMOV. Anything particular you fancy, sir?

GLOUMOV. No, no, get another bottle of vodka in case Madame Maniefa comes in.

STYOPKA. You couldn't let me have something off that 400 roubles, could you?

GLOUMOV. Put down a tip for yourself on the account.

STYOPKA. Thanks very much, sir.

Going to a mirror on the wall he combs his hair, fixes it in a becoming manner with the aid of saliva, and, while GLOUMOV *and his mother continue talking, ambles out.*

MADAME G. Well, I'm going.

Making for the door.

GLOUMOV. Mamma, just a minute, come here. Are you bosom friends with Madame Tourousina's "companions"?

MADAME G. More or less.

GLOUMOV. And the servants and pilgrims, the whole of the ménage?

MADAME G. Oh yes, they tell me anything.

GLOUMOV. Well, don't leave anything to chance. On your way there you'd better buy two snuff boxes for Matriosha and Lubinka.

MADAME G., *starting to go.* All right, I will.

GLOUMOV. And don't forget to keep an eye on everybody who comes into the house. Watch for any suspicious characters from our point of view.

MADAME G. All right. Good-bye.

GLOUMOV. Good-bye. And for heaven's sake get them to hurry up with the reception.

MADAME G. Which reception?

GLOUMOV. Don't be stupid, Mamma. For the formal announcement of the engagement.

MADAME G. They say it can't be for another two weeks at least.
She goes. GLOUMOV *reads through his diary, chuckling wryly to himself once or twice. Then he says to himself.*

GLOUMOV. Let's see, what was I going to put in? Oh yes, the expenses.
Writing.
Two snuff boxes for Matriosha and Lubinka.
There is a knock at the front door. GLOUMOV *answers it and* KROUTITZKY *appears.*
Oh! . . . come in, Mr. Kroutitzky. This is an honour.

KROUTITZKY, *entering.* The paper's waiting for my article. They must have it this morning.

GLOUMOV, *getting some papers from a drawer.* It's all ready. I hope you'll find it satisfactory.
Indicating the room.
We live very humbly, I'm afraid.
Handing him the papers.
Here.

KROUTITZKY, *studying the first page*. Excellent, bravo! A good round hand, thoroughly legible. "Treatise" though, I don't like that. It should be "plan".

GLOUMOV. Well, I thought the word "plan" gave the impression that you were suggesting something new. Whereas the whole point of the article is that you're opposed to anything new.
With ingratiating smile.
And quite rightly so.

KROUTITZKY. So you think "treatise" is better?

GLOUMOV. Much.

KROUTITZKY. Very well.
Reads.
"A Treatise on the Betterment of the Russian Peoples by the Immediate Abolition of all Progressive Ideas." Don't you think that "all" is perhaps a little strong?

GLOUMOV. But that's the theme of your article, isn't it, Mr. Kroutitzky? That all reforms, all progressive ideas are harmful?

KROUTITZKY. I'm not against infinitesimal changes here and there.

GLOUMOV. In that case they wouldn't be reforms, they'd be modifications.

KROUTITZKY. True, true, most penetrating. I'm very pleased with you, young man. You should go far.

GLOUMOV. Thank you, Mr. Kroutitzky.

KROUTITZKY, *putting on his spectacles*. Well, to continue, I'm most interested to see how you've commenced the exposition of my principle thesis.
Reads.
"Every progressive idea is harmful. What is a progressive idea? It is a poisoned arrow aimed at the vitals of the state. How is a progressive idea translated into action? (*a*) By the abolition of something old. (*b*) By the introduction of something new. Which of these two actions is harmful? Both are equally harmful. By sweeping away the old we

create an opportunity for the dangerous keenness of the human brain to penetrate the reasons why this or that is being swept away and to come to the following conclusions: only useless things are swept away; if a certain institution has been abolished, it must have been useless. Such conclusions inevitably lead to dissatisfaction with the existing state of affairs and would bring about discussions in which the government of the country might be criticised. It is clear, therefore, that progressive ideas can only be viewed with abhorrence by anyone who has the welfare of his country at heart."

GLOUMOV. And quite true, Mr. Kroutitzky.

KROUTITZKY, *reading again.* "In admitting a new idea we are making an unnecessary concession to the so-called spirit of the times, which is nothing but the invention of idle brains." Very well expressed.

GLOUMOV. I take no credit for that. It's your fundamental truths which create my style.

KROUTITZKY. You think these are fundamental truths?

GLOUMOV. But there's no question of it.

KROUTITZKY. Yes, I think this should prove very popular.

GLOUMOV. I have to apologise for something—there are several words and expressions which I've left exactly as you wrote them.

KROUTITZKY. Oh, yes?

GLOUMOV. I thought our modern way of writing too weak to express the full splendour of your thoughts.

KROUTITZKY. For instance? . . . Give me an example.

GLOUMOV. Well . . . the passage about the position of minor officials in the Civil Service.

KROUTITZKY. Yes?

GLOUMOV. You most forcibly express the excellent idea that on no account should minor officials have their salaries raised, nor their living conditions improved. That, on the contrary, it's the heads of the departments and ministers who should have their salaries raised.

KROUTITZKY, *turning over the papers.* I don't recall saying that.

GLOUMOV. You *did,* Mr. Kroutitzky. I know the paragraph by heart and not only that but the whole article.

KROUTITZKY. Excellent. Well, tell me what I said in this paragraph.

GLOUMOV. "The raising of Civil Servants' salaries should be carried out with the greatest care and must only be granted to heads of departments and ministers, in no case to minor officials and clerks. The salaries of important officials should be raised so that the power of the state may be upheld with all due pomp and majesty. No subordinate Civil Servant must be contented or well-fed, as this might lead to his acquiring a dignity and self-respect wholly out of keeping with the station to which God has called him. This applies equally to workers of all classes."

KROUTITZKY. Quite right, quite right.

GLOUMOV. I thought the expression "pomp and majesty" most felicitous.

KROUTITZKY, *now engrossed in the article.* Have you shown this to your cousin, your uncle as you call him?

GLOUMOV. Mr. Mamaev?

KROUTITZKY. Yes.

GLOUMOV. Good heavens, no!

KROUTITZKY. Well, look out. He pretends to be intelligent but the man's a complete idiot.

GLOUMOV. I wouldn't argue with you on that point, Mr. Kroutitzky.

KROUTITZKY. He's always telling people how to do things but let him try to write something—we'd soon see. And I wouldn't say his wife was remarkable for her brains.

GLOUMOV. I wouldn't argue on that point either.

KROUTITZKY. How you manage to get on with them I can't understand!

GLOUMOV. It's simply a case of necessity.

KROUTITZKY. Are you in the Civil Service?

GLOUMOV. Not yet, but my aunt spoke to Ivan Gorodoulin about me.

KROUTITZKY. What a man to go to! A fine sort of post you'll get from him. Surely you want something permanent. All these Gorodoulin posts won't last long—you'll soon see. We consider him extremely dangerous.

GLOUMOV. It's not a newly created post though. Nothing progressive about it.

KROUTITZKY. In that case it's not so bad. You should accept it for the time being. Later, you must get transferred to St. Petersburg—things are much better there—I'll give you some letters of introduction. I suppose you've a perfectly clean record?

GLOUMOV, *round-eyed.* A clean record, Mr. Kroutitzky?

KROUTITZKY. I must be able to recommend you in all good faith. Is there anything in your past that——

GLOUMOV. I was very lazy at the University, I'm afraid.

KROUTITZKY. That's all to the good. Far worse if you'd learnt too much. Isn't there anything more important?

GLOUMOV. I—I hardly like to tell you, Mr. Kroutitzky.

KROUTITZKY, *sternly.* Come on, better make a clean breast of it.

GLOUMOV. I was very young at the time—I was easily infatuated, sometimes indiscreet.

KROUTITZKY. Don't be afraid to tell me.

GLOUMOV. I didn't behave like these—these progressively minded students nowadays.

KROUTITZKY. What do you mean?

GLOUMOV. I—I confess I spent some rather riotous evenings. I sowed one or two wild oats. I've sometimes even been in scraps with the police.

KROUTITZKY. Is that all?

GLOUMOV. All, Mr. Kroutitzky? I sincerely hope so.

KROUTITZKY. Well, I like the sound of this. Any young fellow at a university is expected to get drunk and smash up a few things occasionally and get in trouble with the police. It's not as if you came from the lower classes. Now I can be quite easy in my mind about you. Frankly, you have made a good impression on me from the start and I can tell you now I've spoken very highly of you in a certain quarter.

GLOUMOV. Yes, Madame Tourousina told me. I—I can hardly find words to tell you how grateful I am.

KROUTITZKY. Have you proposed yet? There's a lot of money attached to the niece.

GLOUMOV. I'm so stupid about money, Mr. Kroutitzky. But I'm quite enchanted with Mashenka.

KROUTITZKY. Well, I couldn't tell you about that. They're all the same to me. I know the aunt's a terrible humbug.

GLOUMOV. Nobody believes in true love nowadays, but I do. I know it exists, Mr. Kroutitzky. I've felt it in my own heart.

KROUTITZKY. You mustn't give way to it. That's a fatal mistake. I was foolish enough to give way once. It happened about forty years ago. I nearly died of love. I was staying in Omsk at the time. . . . Why are you looking at me like that?

GLOUMOV. I was feeling for you, Mr. Kroutitzky. I know what you must have suffered.

KROUTITZKY. Yes, I was in a terrible state. They thought I had scarlet fever. Well . . . a young man like you deserves the best out of life. We'll soon find you an important position. We need men of your sort. Although you're a youngster I consider that you're one of us. Your support will be invaluable in combating this new wave of dangerous thinking. Anyway, my dear fellow, how much do I owe you for your work?

GLOUMOV. Please, Mr. Kroutitzky, I shall be offended.

KROUTITZKY. No, no, tell me or *I* shall be offended.

GLOUMOV. Well, I wouldn't dream of taking money from you but if you insist there is something you could do for me.

KROUTITZKY. What's that?

GLOUMOV. Marriage is such a tremendous step for a man to take ... I beg you not to refuse me. The blessing of a person like yourself would be a—a kind of guarantee of happiness. ... Even to know you, Mr. Kroutitzky, is a happiness in itself and the idea of a relationship, even though it were only spiritual, would mean such a tremendous lot to ... to any children Mashenka and I may have.

KROUTITZKY. You want me to be godfather to your children, is that the idea?

GLOUMOV. Oh, Mr. Kroutitzky, if you only would!

KROUTITZKY. Of course, why not? There's nothing so wonderful in that. You should have asked me straight out.

GLOUMOV. Oh, but it *is* wonderful, too wonderful. May I tell Madame Tourousina?

KROUTITZKY. Tell her by all means.
Looking at his watch.
We've been sitting here talking and the articles should have been at the Moscow Gazette half an hour ago.

GLOUMOV. My servant's out I'm afraid. Let me get a cab and take it down myself.

KROUTITZKY, *handing it to him.* There's a good fellow. And, look here, as you know, it's to be published anonymously, so don't say a word about it to anyone. If there's any discussion as to who wrote it you pretend you don't know.

GLOUMOV. I promise you I shan't breathe a word.

KROUTITZKY. Hurry up then, I'll make my own way down. I haven't got young legs like you.

GLOUMOV. Very well.
Fervently.
I can never thank you enough for what you've done for me.

KROUTITZKY. I'm indebted to you, too. Goodby.
GLOUMOV bows and taking the papers hurries out. Left to himself KROUTITZKY has a good look round the room, then taking his hat, adjusts his tie in the mirror preparatory to

going out. There is a light tap on the door and KLEOPATRA
MAMAEVA *roguishly puts her head round. On seeing* KROU-
TITZKY *her face falls.*

KLEOPATRA. Oh! . . . What are you doing here?
She comes into the room.

KROUTITZKY. I called to see your young cousin.
Kissing the hand which she extends to him.
How are you, my dear lady?

KLEOPATRA. Where's Yegor?

KROUTITZKY. He'll be back presently . . . if you'll excuse me I
was just on my way out.

KLEOPATRA, *seating herself. Coyly.* No, you must stay and
talk to me. You are an unchivalrous old gentleman! Aren't
you interested in young ladies any more?

KROUTITZKY, *laughing waggishly.* No, no, my day's over, I'm
afraid. Though in my time I had the reputation for—
stops short.
well, I think it's time I made way for the young men.

KLEOPATRA. But they're worse than the old ones nowadays.

KROUTITZKY. Now come, a charming woman like you. . .

KLEOPATRA. They're very disappointing.

KROUTITZKY, *seating himself.* Yes, there are no noble feelings,
no poetic flights of passion nowadays. Shall I tell you the reason? They don't give enough tragedies in the theatres. If
only they'd revive the plays of Ozeroff. Young people of
today would assimilate those fine, delicate feelings. Yes,
they should give tragedies much oftener, every other night
say. I've been working on a plan for spiritually uplifting
the younger generation. I prescribe Ozeroff's tragedies for
the upper classes and for the lower classes, cheaper beer. In
my time we knew all the tragedies by heart, but nowadays!
They don't even know how to read them. That's why we
had chivalry and fine feelings in our time and today they're
only interested in money.
He recites.
"Must I wait for fate to cut short my days, when those days
are so lacking in laughter?" Do you remember?

KLEOPATRA, *acidly.* Yes, of couse I remember. Fifty years ago. I would remember, wouldn't I?

KROUTITZKY. I'm so sorry. Do forgive me. I always look upon you as my contemporary. . . . Oh, I was going to say, I'm very taken with your young cousin. A most delightful young fellow.

KLEOPATRA. I think so, too.

KROUTITZKY. But you musn't spoil him.

KLEOPATRA. Spoil him?

KROUTITZKY. Wait a minute, I think I've remembered some more.
Recites.
"Oh, Gods! 'Tis not the gift of oratory I crave, but for the language of the heart and soul."

KLEOPATRA. How do I spoil him?

KROUTITZKY. Well, arranging such a fine marriage. What a charming girl she is, too.

KLEOPATRA. Charming girl? What . . .
She is unable to go on but sits gaping at him, while he continues to recite.

KROUTITZKY.
Oh Mother, dry your flow of tears,
And sister hide your signs of grief.

KLEOPATRA. What girl? What are you talking about? Whom do you mean?

KROUTITZKY. Good heavens! Mashenka, of course. Sophia Tourousina's niece. As if you didn't know! Twenty thousand dowry.

KLEOPATRA, *getting to her feet.* Oh, my God, I can't believe it! It's not true. . . .

KROUTITZKY, *intent on remembering lines from his favourite tragedy.*
Your soul was sick when you heard the news
And you hid in your breast your sighs,
But gloomy grief is upon your brow,
And . . .

KLEOPATRA. Oh, stop, stop! I shall go mad with this awful re-
citing!

KROUTITZKY. Yes, the boy seems to have a heart, too. "Don't
think it's for money, Mr. Kroutitzky," he said. He asked me
to become godfather to his children. "It would be such an
honour for them," he said. Well, why not? "It's not because
of her dowry," he said, "I really love the girl. She's an angel,
an angel." And he said it with such feeling. It did my heart
good. Do you remember those marvellous lines in Donskey,
"When a Russian gives his word, only death can break his
pledge"?

KLEOPATRA, *groaning.* Oh! . . .

KROUTITZKY. What? What's the matter?

KLEOPATRA. Oh, I'm ill. It's migraine. It's . . .

KROUTITZKY. Oh, you'll soon get over that. Do you remember
that beautiful line, "Thou accusest me, my rival, of betrayal
of thy woman"?

KLEOPATRA, *screaming.* Oh, go away, go away! I shall go mad,
I can't stand it!

KROUTITZKY. My dear lady, I——

KLEOPATRA. Go away! Leave me alone, go, go!
KROUTITZKY *takes one look at her and runs, with a frightened
glance over his shoulder.* KLEOPATRA *collapses on the nearest
chair.*
Oh, my God, I can't believe it! Oh . . . Oh! . . .
After a minute or two she pulls herself together.
Perhaps it's a mistake. . . . Oh, if only I knew.
Looking round the room.
I wonder if there's something here, some love letters per-
haps.
She starts to search, muttering between her sobs.
I'll do something dreadful to him if it's true. I will, I will!
Oh God, pray that it's not! It's that wicked Old Kroutitzky
making mischief!
Opening the drawer.
What's this? . . . His diary? . . .
Hearing footsteps she quickly replaces the diary, shuts the

*drawer and wiping away her tears, forces herself to appear
composed.* GLOUMOV *comes in. He stops short on seeing her.*

GLOUMOV. Kleopatra! What a wonderful surprise! Is it really
you sitting here in my poor little humble home like a god-
dess descended from the skies?

KLEOPATRA. I came to call on your mother.

GLOUMOV. You've just missed her. She went out a few moments
ago.

KLEOPATRA. What a pity.

GLOUMOV, *bringing forward a chair for her.* Do sit down. You're
going to stay and talk to me, aren't you? Kleopatra, you
look unhappy. Are you worried about something?

KLEOPATRA, *sitting down.* About someone.

GLOUMOV. Who is it? Anyone who could make you unhappy
must be a black-hearted wretch!

KLEOPATRA. Yes he is, that's what he is, a black-hearted wretch.

GLOUMOV. Well, as I'm neither black-hearted nor a wretch,
it means that——

KLEOPATRA. That what?

GLOUMOV. That at least it can't be me.

KLEOPATRA. Can I really believe that?

GLOUMOV. You must believe it.

KLEOPATRA. Oh, I want to, I want to! . . .

GLOUMOV. Look into my eyes. Can't you see there that I'd
rather die than cause you a moment's pain? Until I met you
I was a shy, timid boy, uncertain of myself, always troubled
with longings and desires which you, and you alone, have
taught me to understand. I was so lonely that I thought I'd
lose my reason sometimes and always I was searching,
searching for the one woman in the world on whom I could
pin my dreams and hopes. But I was poor, insignificant and
women turned away from me. And then I met you. I shall
never forget the first time I saw you—you were wearing
that beautiful pink dress with brown bows on. My heart
missed a beat and then started to pound so violently that I

thought I should faint. You were so young, so beautiful, so far, far above me! . . . When we were introduced I hardly dared to speak. But you didn't turn away, you weren't cold and cruel like the other great society ladies of today, you were sweet and gracious and when I told you I loved you, Kleopatra, you listened. Oh, if you only knew how many times your sweet, gentle smile has stopped me on the very brink of impropriety. But even that day when I forgot myself, you didn't turn me from the house! Oh, my God, what happiness you've given me.

Feverishly kissing her hands.

What happiness, what happiness!

KLEOPATRA. When are you going to be married?

GLOUMOV, *sitting up with a start.* Married? . . . I . . . er . . . what do you mean?

KLEOPATRA. I understand you're getting married.

GLOUMOV, *after a pause.* I—I must explain it to you, Kleopatra. I was going to tell you today. . . . I'm in a terrible dilemma. Your husband wants me to marry. It was his idea. But I loathe the very thought of it.

KLEOPATRA. He must be fond of you, to want to make you happy against your will!

GLOUMOV. It's simply a question of money. He hates the idea of my being poor. He wants to see me independent and comfortably situated instead of just a poor nobody. It all comes from the goodness of his heart, but unfortunately he didn't consult my feelings.

KLEOPATRA. Do you like the young woman he's chosen for you?

GLOUMOV. She's repugnant to me. Any woman is, but you!

KLEOPATRA. So you don't love her?

GLOUMOV. How could I? But I daren't show her, of course. Whom should I deceive, her or you?

KLEOPATRA. Both, perhaps.

GLOUMOV. You're torturing me with your suspicions! I can't bear it. I shall stop the whole thing.

KLEOPATRA. Stop it? How?

GLOUMOV. Let Uncle be angry with me! I will not marry that girl! I shall tell him so!

KLEOPATRA. Do you mean that?

GLOUMOV. I shall tell him today.

KLEOPATRA. Oh, you must! . . . Without love, whatever sort of marriage would it be?

GLOUMOV. And to think you thought so badly of me! . . . Aren't you ashamed of yourself?

KLEOPATRA. Yes, I've misunderstood you. I'm ashamed.

GLOUMOV, *passionately*. I'm yours, yours, you know that, Kleopatra! Only don't breathe a word to uncle or anyone, or you might give yourself away. Just leave everything to me.

KLEOPATRA. Of course, of course.

GLOUMOV. It's all come about through my cursed shyness. I was afraid to tell uncle straight out that I wouldn't marry. I just went on saying, "Well, let's see . . . there's no hurry," and so on. And this is what's come of it.

The front door bell rings.

Who's that? I expect it's someone to see me. Kleopatra, you must be exhausted with all these fearful emotions. Would you like to go and lie down in Mother's room? I'll get rid of the visitors as quickly as I can.

Leading the way, KLEOPATRA *following him.*

KLEOPATRA. Thank you, Yegor. I couldn't bear to face anybody now.

GLOUMOV *opens the front door disclosing* GOLUTVIN.

GLOUMOV, *rudely*. Well?

GOLUTVIN. Firstly, this is hardly the way to receive a guest. And, secondly, I'm tired because I walked here.

He pushes his way past GLOUMOV *into the room.*

GLOUMOV. What do you want?

GOLUTVIN. Twenty-five roubles minimum. You can make it more if you like. I shan't be offended.

GLOUMOV. Look here, who gave you the idea I was a charitable institution?

GOLUTVIN. I'm not asking for charity. I've done a lot of work on your account and I expect to be paid for it.

GLOUMOV. What work?

GOLUTVIN. Writing your biography.

GLOUMOV. What are you talking about?

GOLUTVIN. I've followed you, watched you, collected information about you and your past history, I've described your latest activities with a wealth of interesting detail and unless you care to buy the manuscript from me I shall send it to the Moscow Weekly Chatterbox with your portrait enclosed. You see, I'm not asking much for it. I don't put a high value on my literary work.

GLOUMOV. Very well, publish it! Don't think you can intimidate *me*. Do you think anyone will want to read what *you* write!

GOLUTVIN. But it's not as if I was asking a thousand roubles. I know I can't do you very much harm but it might be quite unpleasant, so why not pay?

GLOUMOV. There's a very ugly word for what you're trying to do.

GOLUTVIN. Do you consider it less honest than sending anonymous letters?

GLOUMOV. What letters? How can you prove it?

GOLUTVIN. No need to get excited. All I'm asking for is twenty-five roubles.

GLOUMOV. Not one kopeck.

GOLUTVIN. You're marrying a rich young woman. Suppose she were to read your biography and say, oh! . . . much simpler to pay up instead of quarrelling with me. I'd be able to eat for a week and you could have peace of mind. Really, I'm asking very little.

GLOUMOV. And suppose I do pay? That wouldn't be the end of it.

GOLUTVIN. I give you my word it would. What do you take me for?

GLOUMOV, *going to the door and opening it.* Get out, go on.

GOLUTVIN. Very well, in the very next issue——

GLOUMOV. Whichever issue you like!

GOLUTVIN, *after a pause.* Well, look here, what about making it twenty roubles? That's not much.

GLOUMOV. Not one kopeck.

GOLUTVIN. All right then, have it your own way. . . . Haven't got a cigarette, have you?

GLOUMOV. No. Do you mind getting out of here?

GOLUTVIN. When I feel like it. I'll have a rest first.
  Sits.

GLOUMOV. Who sent you here? Kourchaev?

GOLUTVIN. Oh no, we've quarrelled. I've finished with him.

GLOUMOV. I asked you to get out.
  GOLUTVIN *gets up, goes to the door leading into the bedroom and peers in.*

GOLUTVIN. What have you got in there?

KLEOPATRA, *from inside.* Who's that? What is it?

GLOUMOV, *pushing* GOLUTVIN *away and pulling the door to.* I give you one minute.

GOLUTVIN. Mm. Madame Mamaeva. Most interesting.

GLOUMOV, *threateningly.* Are you going?

GOLUTVIN, *sauntering out.* You're such a rotten character yourself that you can't recognise decent feelings in other people. . . .
  By this time he is in the hall.

GLOUMOV. Just a minute, I want a word with you.
  He hurries after him, closing the living-room door. KLEOPATRA *puts her head round the other door.*

KLEOPATRA. That's funny. Who was that, I wonder?
  Suddenly recollecting.
  The diary!

Running to the desk, she pulls open the drawer and takes the diary out.

Perhaps there's something about me—or Mashenka. . . .

Turns the pages.

Here's something. "Mashenka is enchanting. What a relief after poor old Auntie Kleo who looks exactly like a horse." Oh! . . . Oh my God! Oh, I feel ill, I'm going to faint! Oh, how low, how low of him! I'll never forgive him, never. I'll make him pay for it. Oh, to think he should have done this to me.

Tearfully.

But he can't mean it. I don't look like a horse, I know I don't! Neel Fedoseitch doesn't think I look like a horse. . . . There's no humiliation bad enough for him. . . . I'll have him crawling back to me on his knees and begging forgiveness, that's what I'll do.

Looking down at the diary.

Yes, and I can, too, with this.

Hides the diary in her bag, then, as she hears the outer door closing.

Oh my God, I mustn't let him see anything. I must keep calm.

GLOUMOV, *coming in.* A most impossible person.

KLEOPATRA. Who was it?

GLOUMOV. I'll throw him down the stairs next time. He's written an abusive article about me and he had the cheek to come here demanding money. Says he'll have it published otherwise.

KLEOPATRA. How horrible. What horrible people there are in the world. Who is this man?

GLOUMOV. Why do you want to know?

KLEOPATRA. Well, it's best to be warned about people like that.

GLOUMOV. Alexander Golutvin his name is.

KLEOPATRA. Where does he live?

GLOUMOV. I don't know; but one could easily find out. Why?

KLEOPATRA. Well, suppose someone were to affront me—it

would be a way of revenging myself. What else can a woman do? We can't fight duels.

GLOUMOV. You're joking, aren't you?

KLEOPATRA. Yes, of course. Did you give him any money?

GLOUMOV. Only a few roubles. Still, I feel easier in my mind now.

KLEOPATRA. But suppose one of your enemies were to give him more?

GLOUMOV. Enemies? I haven't any.

KLEOPATRA. Then you've nothing to worry about. Poor dear boy, has he upset you?

GLOUMOV. Oh, I'm not worried about him.

KLEOPATRA. What is it then?

GLOUMOV. I'm still miserable at the thought of your mistrusting me.

KLEOPATRA. Have you quite made up your mind not to marry Mashenka?

GLOUMOV. You know I have.

KLEOPATRA. You realise fully what you're giving up?

GLOUMOV. Money. I can do without that if it means losing you.

KLEOPATRA. It's a lot of money though. Twenty thousand, don't forget.

GLOUMOV. Do you think I'd change you for all the wealth in the world?

KLEOPATRA. You really mean it?

GLOUMOV. With all my heart.

KLEOPATRA. You're a truly noble character, Yegor, there's no doubt about that. Come here and let me kiss you.

GLOUMOV *obediently comes over and kneels before her. She puts her hands on his neck as if she would like to strangle him, then kisses him violently as though inflicting a punishment. Suddenly she stops, leaving* GLOUMOV *gasping.*

I must go now. Your uncle will wonder what has happened to me. . . . Goodby, dear Yegor.

GLOUMOV. Kleopatra! . . . When shall I see you again?

KLEOPATRA. I shall expect you this evening.

GLOUMOV, *following her.* Don't think any more of Mashenka. By that time it will all be arranged.

KLEOPATRA, *turning to the door.* Goodby.

GLOUMOV. Until this evening. . . .

She holds out her hand to be kissed; as he kisses it she lowers it abruptly so that he has to bow almost to the ground. Pulling it away, she hurries out.

GLOUMOV, *when her footstps have died away.* Phew! . . . Thank God that's over. . . . Oh well, I'd better get off to see Mashenka.

On his way to the table, he stops short and says.

Let's see, Golutvin's paid off . . . Kleopatra's all right for the moment.

His spirits beginning to rise.

Things aren't going too badly. I'll be able to bring it off with a bit of luck. . . .

Looking round the room.

Now let's see, what am I looking for? I'm becoming quite absent-minded with all these worries. Hat and gloves, that's it . . . now I wonder if I've got everything . . . er . . . wallet in this pocket, diary in that. . . . Oh! . . .

Discovering it's not there.

Where did I put it? . . . the desk of course.

Pulls open the drawer and stops dead.

That's funny, I swear I put it in there. My God, this is terrible! . . .

Starts to search frantically.

I know I put it in the desk, I remember now . . . if she's stolen it, this'll finish everything.

Then a sudden thought strikes him.

I wonder if Golutvin took it.

He continues to search again.

What a fool, what a fool to have left it lying about like that. Why didn't I lock the drawer? Oh my God, it *has* gone, it *has.*

Collapsing on a chair, he holds his head in his hands, then after a moment.

What on earth did I keep it for? It's not as if I had any heroic deeds to record . . . simply out of foolish, childish spite—The Memoirs of a Scoundrel written by himself. . . .

Pause.

Well, it's no good reproaching myself now. I've got enough reproaches coming from everybody else.

Clutching his head.

God, let me think! There must be some way out.

After a moment.

If it's Golutvin I can always get it back with money. . . . Yes, I'll have to buy it back. But suppose it's Kleopatra? "—no fury like a woman scorned." Oh good God, and I said she looked like a horse!

Another pause, during which he takes in the full horror of the situation.

I mustn't be defeated. I won't be. I won't be! Not at this stage. . . . I wonder if she's planning some horrible revenge?

Suddenly making up his mind.

There's only one thing to do.

Gets up resolutely, takes his hat and gloves and adjusts his hat at a becoming angle in the mirror.

Yes, Kleopatra Mamaeva, I'm not going to be defeated by you, or Mr. Golutvin . . . so here we go, straight into the lioness's jaws! And heaven help me to explain that bit about the horse!

He squares his shoulders and hurries out.

Curtain

ACT THREE

The same as Act two, Scene 1. It is late afternoon. The French windows on to the garden are flung open. KOUR-CHAEV *and* MASHENKA *are talking, he seated, she pacing the room restlessly.*

KOURCHAEV. Well, I can't understand the thing at all.

MASHENKA. Neither can I. . . . It all happened so suddenly. . . . Do you think it could possibly be some deep-laid plot?

KOURCHAEV. Perhaps there is something in these queer superstitions of your aunt's.

MASHENKA. I've given up trying to understand. I feel dazed by it all.

KOURCHAEV. I've known him for years. I never noticed anything very special about him. I lost my temper with him once recently, when I thought he'd been running me down to my uncle, but it was just my hot-headedness. He's much too decent to have done a thing like that.

MASHENKA. One moment we weren't aware of his existence and the next he'd become the most important thing in our lives. Ever since then auntie's companions invariably see him in their dreams; whenever they tell fortunes he comes out in the cards; even the professional fortunetellers who come here keep seeing visions of a fair young man named Yegor, and those horrid old pilgrims do, too. And then as the finishing touch, Madame Maniefa, whom I don't like a bit because she always smells of rum, but whom auntie looks upon practically as a saint, described his appearance in detail although she'd never set eyes on him, and foretold the exact moment when he'd arrive at the house. And I've no answer to it all. I can't go against auntie's wishes and she's become absolutely devoted to him.

KOURCHAEV, *gloomily.* It all comes of my not leading a better life. Now Gloumov will get you—and the money too. Virtue will be rewarded and vice punished—vice being me. All I can do is quietly to disappear. If it were some bounder who was getting you I'd put up a fight, but when it's a decent chap like Gloumov I don't see how I can.

MASHENKA. Ssh, they're coming. Oh, I don't want to see him now.

She runs out and KOURCHAEV *jumps to his feet as* GLOUMOV *and* MADAME TOUROUSINA *enter from the garden.*

GLOUMOV. You see, as soon as I realised what a deep longing I had for a settled family life, I took the matter very seriously. Nothing is more abhorrent to me than the idea of marrying for money. Turning what should be a sacred institution into a business transaction. The alternative is to marry for love—but even love is too much of this world. No, I believe a true marriage must come from something higher than all this. It must be dictated by some mystic decree of fate——

MADAME T. Yes, Yes, that's what I always say!

GLOUMOV. By the mysterious powers lurking in the air, with whom we can make contact if we only have intelligence enough to try.

MADAME T. Yes, we can, we can! I entirely agree with you.

GLOUMOV. All my life I've fought against this horrible, radical free-thinking that decries everything mystic or occult—to me, the only things that matter in the world.

MADAME T. Yes, yes, exactly! That's just what I say!

GLOUMOV. I've always believed in miracles——

MADAME T. So have I, always! How right you are.

GLOUMOV. —and I realised that the only way to discover the one woman who'd been waiting for me since the beginning of time, was through a miracle. I prayed for one—and it happened.

MADAME T. It was! It *was* a miracle, your coming here that day! I've always said so. Do you know Yegor, you're the only young man in Moscow who thinks as I do? Everywhere one looks one sees nothing but hideously-minded liberals.

Glancing at KOURCHAEV *who bows. She turns to* GLOUMOV *again.*

But do go on, Yegor. This miracle, tell me about it.

GLOUMOV. Well, I went to a wonderful clairvoyante I know of.

MADAME T. Madame Maniefa?

GLOUMOV. Who? No, I've never heard of her. It was someone quite different. Anyway, as soon as I entered the room, before I'd uttered a word, before she'd even had time to glance at me—she was sitting with her back to me, as a matter of fact—she said, "It's you who are looking for a wife. It's they who are looking for you. Go forward with your eyes closed and you will find her."

MADAME T, *gasping.* How extraordinary! What did you say?

GLOUMOV. Well, a most peculiar feeling came over me. I felt just as if I were enveloped in a cloud.

MADAME T. In a cloud? How extraordinary! Madame Maniefa *saw* you in it. You were in this cloud, slowly descending. . . .

GLOUMOV. That's it, as though in a balloon. But I pulled myself together and managed to say, "Where shall I go, show me?" So she said, "You'll enter a strange house. You must search and you will find. They're waiting for you." Well, the very same evening my cousin brought me to you. And you *were* waiting for me.

MADAME T. It's undoubtedly a miracle. If only everyone could know of this. We could start a religious revival.

KOURCHAEV. I remember a case like that in Kiev once. It happened to a ginger-haired fellow. . . .

MADAME T. Why don't you go for a little walk in the garden? KOURCHAEV *bows, hesitates a minute or two, while they continue talking, then goes out.*

GLOUMOV. It's so clearly a case of predestination that I've never even asked you about Mashenka's feelings. It seemed quite enough that she'd given her consent.

MADAME T. That's all that's needed.

GLOUMOV. She may not be in love with me at the moment, but she will be later on.

MADAME T. Of course she will be.

GLOUMOV. It's written in the stars that Mashenka will love me or we'd never have been brought together in this way.

MADAME T. That's exactly what I was going to say.

GLOUMOV. A marriage like ours has nothing to do with ordinary human motives, so it cannot go wrong.

MADAME T. If only everyone in Moscow could hear you speak. You could be a great teacher, we've all something to learn from you, everyone of us, even I.

GRIGORI, *entering.* Mr. Gorodoulin, madam.

MADAME T. Oh, entertain him for a little, will you, Yegor? I feel too exalted to make idle conversation. All right, Grigori, show him in.
GRIGORI *goes, she continues.*
I think I'll go down into the summerhouse and look into the crystal. Perhaps we shall see something today. I thought I saw something yesterday, but when I looked closer it was only an earwig crawling on the other side.
She goes into the garden. GRIGORI *shows in* GORODOULIN.

GORODOULIN. Oh hello, Gloumov.

GLOUMOV. How are you?

GORODOULIN. How much money are you getting?

GLOUMOV. Twenty thousand, I believe.

GORODOULIN. How did you manage it?

GLOUMOV. But you yourself suggested me. Madame Tourousina told me so.

GORODOULIN. What? Oh yes, I remember. . . . But how do you get on with her—an agnostic like you?

GLOUMOV. I just don't argue.

GORODOULIN. Well, what do you say to all her unutterable bosh?

GLOUMOV. Nothing will cure her of it, so why try?

GORODOULIN. Well, you'll be a rich man soon. I'll put you up for membership of my club.

GLOUMOV. Thanks. . . .
Lowering his voice.
Did you know that Kroutitzky's treatise is to be published in a week or two?

GORODOULIN. Good God! Well, I only hope it gets torn to pieces by the press.

GLOUMOV. Nothing could be easier, anyway.

GORODOULIN. You could do it superbly. You're just the man, with your talents. The only thing is that it might do you a lot of harm. Tell you what, why don't you write it and I'll sacrifice myself for you. I'll make out it's by me, purely out of friendship of course. They need showing up, these intolerable old bores.

GLOUMOV. One's only to look at the trash they write.

GORODOULIN. They're figures of fun, and they should be exposed as such. I'd do it myself, only I haven't the time. You know, we need men like you. We've plenty of good business men, of course, but no one who can write or speak well— so when we're attacked by the old gentlemen of Kroutitzky's sort, it's most unfortunate. One or two of the younger men aren't unintelligent but they're too young. If we allowed them to speak they'd get above themselves. No, you can start the chorus and we'll all join in. Where's your fiancée by the way?

GLOUMOV. I think she's in the garden.

GORODOULIN. I'll go and have a chat with her.

GLOUMOV. I'll come out directly. Aunt Kleopatra's coming to see me here and she's perfectly reconciled to my marriage. Don't you think that's charming of her?
GORODOULIN *goes out. There is the sound of voices in the hall.*

GLOUMOV, *going to the door.* Kleopatra! I'm in here.
After a moment, MADAME MAMAEVA *enters.*

KLEOPATRA. Well, have you found it?

GLOUMOV. No. Golutvin vows on the sacred memory of his mother that he didn't take it. He was in tears almost. "I'd rather starve," he said, "than do a dishonest thing like that."

KLEOPATRA. Who could have taken it then? Are you sure you haven't left it somewhere?

GLOUMOV. Absolutely certain.

KLEOPATRA. Perhaps your servant threw it away by mistake.

GLOUMOV. I wish to God he had.

KLEOPATRA. Why? What are you so afraid of people reading?

GLOUMOV. Nothing particular. Only my intimate thoughts. A few love poems. Some tender lines about women's faces. I'm embarrassed at the idea of a stranger reading them.

KLEOPATRA. Well, you needn't worry. Nobody's going to take any notice of love poems and tender lines. Everyone writes diaries like that. But why are you alone? Where's your fiancée?

GLOUMOV. Somewhere about. I'm not interested. . . . There's proof for you, that I'm only marrying for money and position. I can't always rely on my youth to get along. I've got to become a man whom people look up to and respect. Wait till I have my own carriage with a really spanking pair of horses! Nobody notices me now, but then it'll be, "Who's this striking-looking man who's suddenly appeared in Moscow? He must be an American," and everyone will be jealous of you.

KLEOPATRA. Why of me?

GLOUMOV. Because I belong to you.

KLEOPATRA. It'd be much nicer if you could get the money without Mashenka. But at any rate, you'll have a charming young wife.

GLOUMOV. That won't make any difference to me. I've offered my hand to the bride, my pocket for the money, and my heart remains with you.

KLEOPATRA. You're a dangerous person. One listens and listens and in the end one almost believes you.

GLOUMOV. Think how proud you'll feel when I drive up to your house in my beautiful carriage.

KLEOPATRA. You'll often drive up, won't you? . . . Well, go on, you'd better go to your fiancée. You must be with her as much as possible, if only for appearances sake.

GLOUMOV. You see, you're sending me to her yourself.

KLEOPATRA. Yes, go, go.

GLOUMOV *goes out into the garden.*

Yes, my friend, you're rejoicing a little too soon. You won't be so pleased with yourself, when I've finished with you.

KOURCHAEV *strolls in, looking gloomy.*

Where are you going, Yegor?

KOURCHAEV. Home.

KLEOPATRA. Home? You do look sad. Wait a minute! I think I can guess why.

KOURCHAEV *bows and makes for the door.*

No, wait!

He bows and makes for the door again.

Oh, you are a horrid creature! Stay here, I want to talk to you.

KOURCHAEV *waits, but it is quite clear that he is longing to get away.* KLEOPATRA *continues.*

There are a lot of things that you are not aware of.

KOURCHAEV. Please let me go, Auntie Kleopatra.

KLEOPATRA. *I'm* going quite soon. You can see me home.

KOURCHAEV *bows.*

Have you lost your tongue, or something? Listen. Be frank with me. I'm your aunt and I order you to obey me. I know you're in love with Mashenka. Does she love you?

KOURCHAEV *bows.*

I'm sure she does. Well, don't give up hope. Life's full of surprises.

KOURCHAEV. If only she'd had ordinary parents, instead of—

KLEOPATRA. And what's the matter with her aunt?

KOURCHAEV. She's got such queer ideas.

KLEOPATRA. What do you mean?

KOURCHAEV. Well, an ordinary fellow can't live up to them. Particularly if he's in the army.

KLEOPATRA. What can't he live up to?

KOURCHAEV. My education hasn't fitted me for it.

KLEOPATRA. What *are* you talking about?

KOURCHAEV. What Madame Tourousina was trying to find for her niece was a . . .

KLEOPATRA. Well?

KOURCHAEV. I mean, I'd never have thought of it. I wouldn't have known there was such a thing.

KLEOPATRA. As what, what?

KOURCHAEV. I've never heard of . . .

KLEOPATRA. Do explain yourself!

KOURCHAEV. She was looking for a thoroughly chaste and virtuous man.

KLEOPATRA. Well, go on.

KOURCHAEV. I haven't any virtues.

KLEOPATRA. None? So you only have vices.

KOURCHAEV. No more than any other fellow, I mean, not to speak of. I'm just an ordinary fellow. But the idea of looking for an absolutely virtuous fellow. Where could she have found one if it hadn't been for Yegor? He's the only one in the whole of Moscow. Miracles happen to him, he appears in cards, he sees visions. How can a fellow compete with that?

KLEOPATRA. Well, don't go yet. Do what I tell you, wait.
    As MASHENKA *comes in.*
    My dear, congratulations. You look prettier each time I see you. I'm so glad to hear you're so happy.

MASHENKA. Mr. Gloumov's such a noble character that I feel quite frightened. I don't feel I'm worthy of him.

KLEOPATRA. I'm sure you are dear—with your upbringing—your aunt's example always before you.

MASHENKA. I'm very grateful to auntie. But the only virtue I've learned is to do what she tells me.

MADAME TOUROUSINA and KROUTITZKY come in from the garden, deep in conversation.

MADAME T. But why must it be tragedies? Why not comedies? *To the others.*
We're discussing how to bring spirituality to the younger generation.

KROUTITZKY. For the reason that a comedy depicts lowness whereas a tragedy depicts sentiments of the highest order, and that's what they need.

KOURCHAEV and KROUTITZKY bow to each other. KROU-TITZKY kisses MADAME MAMAEVA's hand as MADAME TOUR-OUSINA continues.

MADAME T. Nobody believes in anything today. All I hear is, "Madame Maniefa's a charlatan. Why do you allow her in your house?" I'd only like some of them to hear her. They'd see what a charlatan she was! Well, I'm delighted for her. Now I've taken her up, she'll become the most fashionable clairvoyante in Moscow, and I hope Moscow will be grateful to me.... I consider myself a public benefactress.

KLEOPATRA. Where's your niece's fiancé? I don't see him.

MADAME T. *to* MASHENKA. Where is Yegor?

MASHENKA. He's in the garden with Gorodoulin.

MADAME T. You know, I expected him to be a very exemplary young man, after I'd heard such glowing accounts from my friends, and for other reasons, too, but now that I've come to know Yegor I find he's much more wonderful than anything I dared to hope for.

MAMAEV, *coming in.* Who's this who's so wonderful?

MADAME T. Yegor Gloumov.

MAMAEV. I knew you'd thank me for him. I didn't offer him any other fiancée, I brought him straight to you. I always know the right man for the right job.

MADAME T. It would have been a sin to take him anywhere else.

KROUTITZKY. Yes, Gloumov should go a long way.

KLEOPATRA. With our help, of course.

GRIGORI comes in.

MADAME T. I don't know why so much happiness has been granted to me. Perhaps for my—

to GRIGORI

what do you want? Perhaps for my good deeds.

He hands her an envelope.

What's this?

Opens it.

A newspaper? It must be for someone else.

KLEOPATRA, *taking the envelope.* No, it's for you. Here's the address.

MADAME T. Surely it is a mistake. Who brought it?

GRIGORI. A postman.

MADAME T. Where is he?

GRIGORI. He's gone long ago.

He goes out.

MAMAEV. Here. Give it here. I'll read it and explain it to you.

He takes the envelope and extracts a printed sheet.

What is it? It's a newspaper and yet not a newspaper. It's a page of a newspaper, an article.

MADAME T. But who sent it to me? The editor?

MAMAEV. From some friend I expect.

MADAME T. Well, what's the article about?

MAMAEV. That we shall see. The article's called "How to Become a Success."

MADAME T. That's of no interest to any of us. Leave it.

MAMAEV. We might as well have a look. There's a portrait in the middle. What's it say underneath? . . .

Reads out.

"Portrait of an Ideal Husband." What's this? It's—it's a picture of Yegor! Yegor Gloumov!

KLEOPATRA. May I see? This is most interesting.
She takes the paper from her husband.

MADAME T. Oh, there must be some vile intrigue against him! He's too good for Moscow. The liberals and freethinkers must be plotting against him!
She glares at KOURCHAEV. MAMAEV *also glares at him.*

KOURCHAEV. Are you suggesting it's me? *I* can't draw portraits.
To MAMAEV.
You're the only person I've ever drawn.

MAMAEV. Yes, yes, I know that.

KLEOPATRA. Whoever wrote this article must know Yegor very well: here are all the most intimate details of his life, if they're not inventions.

MAMAEV, *taking* GLOUMOV's *diary from the envelope.* There's something else here.
He opens it.

KROUTITZKY, *peering over his shoulder.* That's Gloumov's handwriting. I know it. I swear it's his.

MAMAEV. Yes, this is his handwriting; but it's someone else's signature on the article. Which shall we read, the article or this?

KROUTITZKY. Let's have the original first.

MAMAEV. Here you are, there's a book-mark in it. We'll start here then. Seems to be a bill. "To Madame Maniefa: twenty-five roubles. To Madame Maniefa: another twenty-five roubles. She's always half-pickled with rum yet takes upon herself to foretell the future. I've spent hours trying to teach her what to say, but it was with the greatest difficulty that I got an ounce of sense out of her. I've also sent her a bottle of rum and given her another twenty-five roubles at least. What a pity that such a profitable profession should be practised by such stupid people. I am curious to know how much she gets from poor Madame T. A great deal I should think, as Madame T. is slightly cracked."

MADAME T., *falling on the couch and feeling for the smelling salts.* Oh! Oh! I can't bear it! I can't bear it!

MASHENKA, *running to her.* It's all right, Auntie. It's best to know now. Mr. Mamaev, please go on.

KLEOPATRA. Yes, go on. It's better for Sophia to know the truth.
MAMAEV *takes a deep breath and continues.*

MAMAEV. "The two nauseating companions have had seven roubles fifty kopecks each, as well as a couple of silver snuff boxes costing ten roubles, in return for which they guarantee to see me in the cards, as well as in their dreams each night."

MADAME T., *suddenly screaming.* They must go at once! I won't have them in the house another minute! Oh my God, this world's too evil to live in. Oh, Mashenka darling, what can one think after this? If one's wicked, one's a sinner, if one's good, one's a fool.

KLEOPATRA. You needn't complain. You're not the only one to be made a fool of.

MAMAEV, *continuing doggedly.* "Six anonymous letters to Madame Tourousina—thirty kopecks."

MASHENKA. So that's where they came from!

MADAME T. Forgive me, forgive me, darling. I should never have attempted to arrange your life. I see now, I've neither the brain nor the strength. Do as you like from now on. Make your own choice. I shall do nothing to stop you.

MASHENKA, *softly.* I've made my choice, Auntie.

MADAME T., *weakly.* At least, darling, you won't be deceived by him; he doesn't pretend to be anything wonderful.
KOURCHAEV *bows.* MADAME TOUROUSINA *suddenly screaming.*
Matriosha and Lubinka must leave the house at once!

KROUTITZKY. To make way for other companions?

MADAME T. I don't know.

MAMAEV. Do you want me to go on?

MADAME T. Yes, go on. Nothing matters now.

MAMAEV. "Mr. Mamaev's servant who brought his master to me, deceitfully taking advantage of the old fellow's weakness for looking over apartments, has received three roubles. A sum well spent, for I hope to get a great deal more than that from the poor old hippopotamus."
Controlling himself with difficulty.
There's no necessity to read any more of this.

KROUTITZKY. Here. Give it to me. I'll read it out.

MAMAEV. That's all right, thanks. I can do it. There's a—a conversation with me here, of no interest to anybody. Ah, this is better. "First visit to the doddering old Kroutitzky."

KROUTITZKY. What? What's that? What?

MAMAEV. "Let's sing the praises of this great old man and his awe-inspiring projects! One cannot admire you enough, venerable aged gentleman. Tell us, only tell us, how you've reached the age of sixty and managed to preserve intact the brain of a six-year-old child."

KROUTITZKY. Enough! Stop! It's a libel! Hand me that book. Give it to me at once.

GORODOULIN *comes in from the garden. Nobody notices him.*

MAMAEV, *struggling for the diary with* KROUTITZKY. Allow me. Please!
Gets it away from him.
Thank you. I see there are a few words about Gorodoulin here. "Gorodoulin was taking part in some idiotic discussion about housing problems the other day, and someone, in a moment of passion, accused him of being a liberal; he was so delighted that for three whole days he drove about Moscow telling everybody he was a liberal. So now he's accepted as one." Well, there you are, that's just like him.

KROUTITZKY. Why don't you read the part about *yourself?* "The poor old hippopotamus," that's you.

GORODOULIN, *coming down to* MAMAEV *and taking the diary from him.* So you think this is just like me?

MAMAEV. Oh . . . er . . . hallo, Ivan. I didn't notice you. Well, so you see what a study's been made of us all?

GORODOULIN. Who is this youthful Juvenal?

MAMAEV. Yegor Gloumov.

MADAME T., *faintly.* Ivan. Take that diary back to its owner and ask him to leave as quietly and quickly as he can.

GLOUMOV comes in from the garden; GORODOULIN *hands him the diary.*

GLOUMOV. Don't alarm yourself, Madame Tourousina. I'm not going to make a fuss, to explain anything, or attempt to justify myself in any way. I should only like to point out that in dismissing me from your society you're making a very big mistake.

KROUTITZKY. We have no use for you, young man. We're decent, honest people here.

General chorus of agreement.

GLOUMOV. Oh. And who has decided that I am dishonest? Was it you, Mr. Kroutitzky? Perhaps your piercing brain became convinced of my dishonesty when I undertook to rewrite your treatise for you? Did you decide that no decent person would agree to do such nauseating work, or did you realise my dishonesty that day in my apartment when I expressed delighted admiration at your most pompously puerile phrases, and fawned upon you so much that I practically licked your boots? Oh no, you were ready to kiss me then, weren't you? What's more, if you'd never got hold of my diary, you'd have looked upon me as a decent honest man until your dying day.

KROUTITZKY. If I hadn't read the diary, yes, but . . .

GLOUMOV. And what about *you,* uncle? When did you decide I wasn't a fit person for your society? When you were teaching me how to flatter Mr. Kroutitzky? Or was it when you gave me a lesson in how to make love to your wife, so as to keep away other admirers, and I blushed and stammered, pretending I didn't know how, and saying I felt ashamed? You knew perfectly well I was pretending, but what did you care, so long as you could fancy yourself as an experienced man of the world teaching an inexperienced youngster how to handle women and get on in life? I'm twenty times more intelligent than you and you know it, but when I pretend to be a fool and ask for your advice you're delighted and prepared to swear that I'm the most honest and decent fellow in the world.

MAMAEV. Well—it's no good bringing up these things now. Better keep quiet about them. We all belong to the same family.

GLOUMOV, *turning to* MADAME TOUROUSINA. I admit I made a fool of you, Madame Tourousina, but I'm not ashamed of that. I'm only sorry for Mashenka. You ask to be made a fool of every day of your life. In fact, you enjoy it. You let a rum-sodden old woman from the streets enter your house and you obediently choose a husband for your niece on that woman's advice. Who does your Madame Maniefa know? Whom can she recommend? The one who gives her the most money, of course. You were lucky it happened to be me and not an escaped convict she saw descending in a cloud. You'd have accepted him in just the same way.

MADAME T. I only know one thing, the world's too evil to live in.

GLOUMOV, *turning to* GORODOULIN. Well, and what about you, Ivan?

GORODOULIN. Not a word. I've the greatest admiration for you. Here's my hand. Every word you've said about us—at least about me, I don't know about the others—is the complete truth.

GLOUMOV. You see, ladies and gentlemen, you all need me. You can't live without a person like me. People much worse than I will come along, and you'll say, "This fellow's worse than Gloumov—but still I can't help liking him. . . ." You're a very staid old gentleman, Mr. Kroutitzky, but when you're with a young man who treats you deferentially and humbly agrees with every word you say—a feeling of rapture goes right through you. You'd do anything to help a man like that. But if he is honest, if he dares to give his true opinion of your futile plans and projects, you'd see him starve before you'd lift a finger for him.

KROUTITZKY. You're taking too great an advantage of our leniency, Mr. Gloumov. You can go too far.

GLOUMOV, *politely.* Don't be offended, please. You can't get on without me, uncle. Even the servants won't listen to your interminable lectures, however much you pay them; whereas I listen to them for nothing.

MAMAEV. That's quite enough. If you haven't understood yet that it's indecent for you to remain here any longer, I must explain it to you.

GLOUMOV. It's quite unnecessary.

Turning to GORODOULIN.

And you're another. You can't get on without me either.

GORODOULIN. I admit it.

GLOUMOV. Where will you get the epigrams for your after-dinner speeches, without me?

GORODOULIN. I've no idea.

GLOUMOV. And how will you write those scathing criticisms without my help?

GORODOULIN. I don't know.

GLOUMOV. And you have need of me too, auntie.

KLEOPATRA. I've nothing to say. There's only one thing I can't forgive you and I'll try to forget that.

KROUTITZKY, *to* MAMAEV. You know, I thought there was something fishy about him from the beginning—

MAMAEV. So did I, something about his eyes.

GLOUMOV. You thought nothing of the sort. You're furious about my diary, that's all. I don't know how it got into your hands, but even the cleverest man makes a slip sometimes. I'd like you to know, ladies and gentlemen, that all the time I was moving in your august society, I was only honest when I was writing in that diary. And any decent person would have the same attitude towards you. Frankly, you make me sick! What's offended you in it, anyway? Surely there's nothing new here. You yourselves constantly say the same things behind each other's backs. If I'd read out to each of you separately what I'd written about the others, you'd have roared with laughter and patted me on the back. I'm the one who should feel offended and furious, not you! I don't know who it was, but it was one of your decent honest members of society who stole my diary. Well, you've ruined everything for me. You're kicking me out, and you think that'll be the end of it. But you're mistaken. You've not heard the end of it, not by any means.

Looking round at them all.

I consider that you've behaved abominably, that your conduct is indefensible and you're not fit to enjoy the society of a decent, honest man like myself.

Turns suddenly, and goes out through the garden. Silence.

MAMAEV. Well . . . er . . . perhaps we oughtn't to let him go like this.

KROUTITZKY. It might be making a mistake.

KLEOPATRA. No, I don't think we ought to let him go.

MADAME T. I'd like to talk to him again. I'm beginning to see things in quite a different light.

GORODOULIN. Let's get him back.

Running to the French windows, he calls.

Yegor! Yegor! Come back!

MAMAEV, *following him.* That's right, call him. He'll hear you. *Yelling.*

Come back, Yegor, come back!

MADAME T. *to* KOURCHAEV. Run after him, stop him before he gets to the gates.

KOURCHAEV *runs out.*

KLEOPATRA, *who has joined the others.* Yegor, come back!

MADAME T., *also joining them, followed by* MASHENKA. I feel I'd like to have a talk with him. He's such an interesting person.

MASHENKA. I don't want to marry him, Auntie, but I agree with everything he said.

MAMAEV. There he is. Kourchaev's catching him up!

ALL, *including* KROUTITZKY, *who has hobbled up in the rear.*
Come back! Yegor, come back, come back!

GRIGORI, *appearing*. Madame Maniefa to see you, madam. . . .
He stands back deferentially to allow her to pass.

Curtain

TOO CLEVER BY HALF
An Afterword by Daniel Gerould

By all accounts Alexander Ostrovsky (1823-1886) is the most important nineteenth-century Russian playwright. In fact, he is the only major Russian author to devote his entire career to the theatre. Pushkin, Lermontov, Gogol, Turgenev, Tolstoi, and Chekhov were primarily poets and novelists, and only sometimes dramatists, whereas Ostrovsky wrote over forty plays, the best of which soon became the basis of a national repertory.

Ostrovsky also immersed himself in the practical side of theatre. He raised the status of his profession by organizing a society of dramatic authors and securing their rights and royalties; he founded a native school of acting in which ensemble playing took precedence over the star system; and he helped to consolidate a nascent realist tradition that found fruition in Stanislavsky and the Moscow Art Theatre. In all these respects Ostrovsky can be considered the most Russian of playwrights.

But here lies the problem. We are told that Ostrovsky is so Russian that he is not easily accessible to Western audiences and cannot be successfully exported for performance on foreign stages. In other words, Ostrovsky's brand of Russianness has not yet been assimilated into the Western theatrical mainstream in the way that Chekhov's has. Now if we ask why this should be so, the answer that we get is that Ostrovsky is a great national author—but not a universal one—because he depicts a social reality so parochially Russian as to be bound to a particular place and time.

Let us look at this argument a little more closely. Son of a well-to-do lawyer who made his fortune representing the increasingly powerful middle class, Ostrovsky grew up in

the mercantile district on the other side of the Moscow River
opposite the Kremlin, and he took as his special province in
most of his plays the uncouth way of life of the nouveau
riche tradesmen, merchants, and petty functionaries—often
the sons of serfs—whom he had known at first hand.

Although, like artists everywhere, the playwright
exaggerated how totally original his discovery of an
uncharted realm actually was—other Russian dramatists had
already made brief forays on the same territory—Ostrovsky
was indeed the first to exploit in depth the picturesque
customs and costumes, bad manners and worse morals of the
un-Europeanized merchant class from "Over-the-River." It
would be fair to say that this was a claustrophobic milieu
dominated by money-grubbers similar in their origins to
Lopakhin from *The Cherry Orchard*, but infinitely cruder
because untouched by the civilizing influence of Madame
Ranevskaya and her circle. Out of this very "raw" material,
Ostrovsky fashioned a gallery of truculent business types, a
veritable human comedy of old patriarchal Russia.

Recognizing the exoticism of this new found land for his
cultured contemporaries, the playwright characterized
"Over-the-River" as "a magic world peopled by creatures as
fantastic as any in the *Arabian Nights*" and likened himself
to the Greek historian Herodotus giving his compatriots
fabulous accounts of Egypt and Babylon. Ostrovsky's
reports seemed so convincingly authentic—although, like
Herodotus's, they were clearly compounded of myth,
making them all the more colorful—that his evocations of
shady speculators, small-time crooks, swindlers, household
tyrants, and con-men seeking heiresses with fat dowries
soon entered into the histrionic consciousness of the Russian
public and still have currency there today.

How could Ostrovsky's highly colored representations of
a grasping, vulgar bourgeoisie that believes only in the
power of the ruble and the absolute right of parents to

browbeat their offspring fail to strike a responsive chord in
the capitalist West? Is it that cut-throat competition,
fraudulent bankruptcies, embezzlement, extortion, black-
mail, bribery, graft, and judicial corruption are only local
Russian matters, unintelligible to foreigners? Granted, the
specific texture of these merchant plays is nineteenth-
century Muscovite, but even so, why should the refined
aristocratic world, with its peasant substratum, depicted by
Turgenev and Tolstoi, seem more familiar to Anglo-
American audiences?

   I would hazard a guess that Ostrovsky's abusive parents,
unsavoury entrepreneurs, mercenary officials, and acquisi-
tive adventurers are perfectly recognizable anywhere, but
that the portraits are not very appealing or flattering; they do
not correspond to popular notions of the "Russian soul,"
derived from reading Russian novels about the upper
classes. Rather than venal and boorish opportunists engaged
in financial speculations, we prefer to accept as a picture of
old Russia sensitive nobles on country estates engaged in
philosophical speculations on the meaning of life.

   Not only does Ostrovsky offer us an alternate
Russianness, but the formal means which he has chosen for
ordering action and dialogue were, by European standards,
unorthodox and idiosyncratic. The conventions of the
well-made play (used, for example, by Ibsen in his portrayal
of a cramped and hypocritical society) may now seem
old-fashioned and obtrusive, but they always serve to render
the material concentratedly dramatic, even overly dramatic.
Ostrovsky, on the other hand, went to an alternate set of
realistic conventions which deliberately disregard dramatic
economy, underplay the very concept of drama, and give the
impression of the unstructured and the unmade. As the
Russian formalist critics have pointed out, this aesthetic
favors such devices as marked elaboration of incidental
characters and inessential details, moving the background to

the fore, preference for disconnected rather than linked scenes, avoidance of expected confrontations and crises, and inconclusive "open" endings that resolve nothing and refuse to conform to the patterns of either comedy or tragedy.

Maintaining that "plot is always something false," Ostrovsky indulges in pictorial expansiveness at the expense of tight-knit sequentiality. As a painter of "scenes from merchant life," the playwright takes no stand, advances no particular moral or philosophical point of view, and remains uncommitted to this or that side of any issue. His dramas are without discernible ideology. According to D.S. Mirsky in his *History of Russian Literature*, this neutrality makes Ostrovsky the least subjective of Russian writers and renders his characters genuine reflections of the "other"—simply "people as seen by other people." Even if this is only an illusion, produced by Ostrovsky's artful mastery of oblique dramatic form, it is a remarkable achievement to have created the impression of a world of human interactions and perceptions, experienced from within a society, without authorial intervention. The absence of manipulation explains, I think, the enduring appeal of the plays for Russian theatre artists; their openness and spatial organization leave room for complex interplay and subtextual explorations by actors and actresses of the sort that Russian ensemble acting made possible.

Of all the specifically Russian qualities of Ostrovsky's dramas, none has been more admired than the language. From the start the playwright was credited with reproducing superbly the speech of the Muscovite merchant caste, and what is more significant, with creating out of this semiliterate vernacular a fluid and colloquial stage idiom, composed of folk sayings, adages, and racy turns of phrase. The belligerent exchanges among Ostrovsky's petty despots contending for power and money are the delight of Russian performers and audiences and the despair of translators. The proverb titles of many of the plays, such as *It's a Family Affair—We'll Settle It Ourselves*; *An Old Friend Is Better Than Two New Ones*; *When your Own Dogs Are Fighting, A Strange Dog Should Not Meddle*; *Not a Kopek, and Suddenly a Ruble*; *Don't Try to Sit in Someone Else's Sleigh*; *A Cat Has Not Always Carnival*; *Your Drink—My Hangover*, are expressive of the collective mentality of the community with its pious superstitions and rough-and-ready folk wisdom. In the mouths of Ostrovsky's charlatans, bullies, and crafty rascals, these sayings are the moralizing of wolves defending their rights to prey on sheep, and should not be taken as the author's judgment. In English, they sound rather like citations from a long tirade by an old Bolshevik politician.

After so many warnings about Ostrovsky's daunting Russianness, we turn to the celebrated *Too Clever By Half* (the author's twenty-seventh play, written in 1868) with a sense of relief that comes from being on familiar ground. Why, we exclaim, here is a delightful play immediately intelligible to a non-Russian public! After all, isn't it a satirical comedy of manners with an ingenious plot that features an impoverished, although nobly born young rogue-hero struggling to make his way to the top by outwitting the powers that be and winning the rich heiress? The plodding, earth-bound merchant quarter has been left behind for the more fashionable and luxurious salons of Moscow where a Westernizing high society vies for positions of pre-eminence. Atypical though it may be in several respects, measured against the author's earlier work, *Too Clever By Half* is, from the Anglo-American perspective, Ostrovsky's most universal play—which simply means that it seems to conform closely to dramatic materials and formulas with which we are acquainted, thereby affording the pleasures of recognition.

But we must not go too far in domesticating the play for

our own uses and denying its distinctive traits as the creation
of Ostrovsky's own dramatical method. It is worth exploring
the familiar, even derivative origins and analogues of *Too
Clever By Half* in order to locate the points of
modification—or "defamiliarization" in formalist
terminology—which give the work its great originality. In
the second half of his career, Ostrovsky made a
rapprochement with more traditional dramatic forms and
techniques. Nowhere else in his work is conscious
theatricalization more evident than in *Too Clever By Half*,
which echoes the patterns of certain well-known comedies
and even "cites" situations and exchanges from several of
these.

Ostrovsky's tale of a hypocritical schemer who feigns
virtue in pursuit of a fortune recalls Sheridan's *School for
Scandal*, which has been performed both in translation and
in a totally Russified version. Like Joseph Surface, Gloumov
has a wealthy uncle to be manipulated and makes advances
to a slightly older lady to gain access to the heiress he hopes
to marry. The innovative difference is that whereas Joseph
has an honest brother, Charles, who embodies the drama's
opposing principle, Gloumov has an honest diary, which
functions as his alter ego.

We may also be reminded of Molière's *Misanthrope*,
from which Ostrovsky has skillfully transposed elements,
alternately making Gloumov an anti-Alceste, who basely
flatters everyone by saying precisely what each interlocutor
wishes to hear, or a crypto-Alceste, reserving his hatred of
society for his secret confidant, the diary which he carries
with him in his pocket. The final scene of exposure in *Too
Clever By Half*, in which each member of the assembled
social group is pilloried by the reading of Gloumov's diary,
has its counterpart in the reading of Célimène's letters in the
fifth act of *The Misanthrope*. In the final moments of the
play, Gloumov, like Alceste, castigates the society that he

now leaves, while others vow to seek his return.

Much closer to Ostrovsky as points of reference for *Too Clever By Half* are the two great Russian comedies of the first half of the nineteenth century, Griboedov's *Woe from Wit* (1823-4) and Gogol's *Inspector General* (1836). In the former, the outspoken young nobleman Chatsky earns the enmity of all by his stinging denunciations of Moscow society, from which he is finally ostracized. In the latter, the impostor Khlestakov, daydreaming of glory, is accidentally mistaken for the inspector general by the inhabitants of a provincial backwater; he is exposed as a fraud only after his departure, when his letter ridiculing the town dignitaries is read aloud. Gloumov combines the roles of the truthful Chatsky and the lying Khlestakov in one and the same person.

The originality—and modernity—of *Too Clever By Half* (a revisionist reading of previous comic protagonists in the same tradition) lies in Gloumov's special nature as both actor and writer. The conflict is not between the young hero and the surrounding world of his client-patrons (his plans for them run smoothly, because his duplicity satisfies their needs), but within Gloumov himself, as he first performs and then records his performance. In the split between his intelligence, capabilities, and powers of observation and the uses to which he must put these talents, there would be a complete betrayal of the self, if it were not for the diary. Gloumov keeps his brains in his pocket. As a superior individual in a mediocre, petty society, he has the choice of either remaining in shabby obscurity or rising by flattery and guile. Ambitious and unscrupulous, Gloumov understands that his gifts as a speaker and writer can be "sold" to a variety of eager takers among the ruling establishment who lack his dynamic ability to direct the course of events.

Gloumov is very much a man of his time. The Great Reforms under Alexander II had been designed to modernize Russia. The emancipation of the serfs in 1861 introduced a market economy and led to the creation of a bourgeois social order. A transitional period full of transitional people, the new capitalist era in Russia favors entrepreneurs and opportunists. Everyone is in a terrible hurry, intent on giving the impression of being busy with important business, and it is crucial to have one's say about the moral development of society and the nature of governmental institutions. The press and "public statement making" (the Russian word used is *glasnost!*) become social obsessions of the post-reform age of economic restructuring. In the struggle of the old and the new, reaction soon sets in and futility and inertia prevail. No wonder bright young go-getters are in demand!

Too Clever By Half is structured as a gallery of satirical portraits of contemporary types, seen largely through Gloumov's eyes (and sketched by his acid pen) as he moves up the social ladder. The construction of the plot is as simple as it is original. At the opening of the play Gloumov does not know personally any of the principal characters and must forge a new circle of acquaintances previously inaccessible to him. These influential people, who are to serve Gloumov only as stepping stones to far higher spheres, belong to the same social clique, although they do not share identical political views and feel distrust and contempt for one another.

Until now ignored as a poor relation Gloumov starts his ascent with his uncle, Mamaev, a middle-grade bureaucrat and wealthy landowner, still outraged at the freeing of the serfs, not due to any financial losses, but because he no longer has a large captive audience for his interminable lectures and must instead harangue shopkeepers and his potential heirs. Through Mamaev, the seemingly obsequious Gloumov meets the retired armchair general, Kroutitzky, who is writing reactionary social tracts on the evils of reform, the influential young official, Gorodoulin, whose current stance is to be for liberal causes, and the rich and bigoted widow of merchant extraction, Tourousina, whose niece, Mashenka (quite as hard-headed and unsentimental as Gloumov) will be the prize.

Nothing out of the ordinary happens. We see the characters engaged in the uneventful daily round of life, talking their usual quota of rubbish, and it is only as reflected in the distorting mirror of Gloumov's mimicry that they achieve a grotesque artistic definition. A linguistic chameleon, the young man with a diary as his prompt-book can imitate perfectly his interlocutors and adopt their mode of expression as well as their way of thinking. With his extraordinary powers of adaptation and his ability to play social roles that are pleasing, Gloumov is an instance of the histrionic temperament—a distinctly modern type of actor-artist in life with a promising future in public affairs.

Writing "On the Problem of the Actor" in 1887 (some twenty years after *Too Clever By Half* first appeared), Friedrich Nietzsche attacks the same issue that Ostrovsky has dramatized in the character: the nature of the histrion and his rise to prominence in the culture of late nineteenth-century European public life. Once there no longer is an immutable social hierarchy where each has a fixed role, individuals discover that they can constitute and reconstitute themselves—then become the masters. According to the German philosopher, the ascendancy of the histrion can be traced to the need for survival and advancement experienced by talented outsiders on the margins of society.

Nietzsche's analysis of "the delight in dissimulation" and "the inner craving to enter a role, to put on a *show*," because of "a surplus of all kinds of adaptiveness that can no longer be satisfied in the service of the most immediate and narrowest utility" applies quite precisely to Gloumov, whose play-acting constantly goes beyond what is necessary for the success of his plan. The actor's art of lying, which Nietzsche calls "falseness with a good conscience," is akin to that of the artist and the diplomat. Gloumov—actor, writer, perhaps future diplomat—practices the perilous calling of "artist" in order "to survive under changing pressures and circumstances."

Like its hero Gloumov, *Too Clever By Half* has shown remarkable adaptiveness during a rich stage history of more than one hundred years since its premiere in 1886 at the Maly Theatre (of which Ostrovsky had just been named managing director). Changing social reality always provides new targets for Ostrovsky's perennially fresh satire, and innovative directors have never hesitated to exploit these topical dimensions. Here I can only mention briefly three of the most celebrated scenic versions.

As staged by Vladimir Nemirovich-Danchenko at the Moscow Art Theatre in 1910—it was maintained in the repertory for the next fifteen years and taken on tour to New York in 1923—*Too Clever By Half* showed an *ancien régime* on the verge of breakdown, vainly propped up by doddering idiots like General Kroutitsky, played as a sinisterly grotesque figure by Stanislavsky, while Vassily Kachalov, who specialized in intellectual heroes and romantic rebels such as Brand, Cain, Hamlet, and Chatsky, transformed Gloumov into a tragicomic virtuoso of simulation, for whom life was a fascinating game. In *My Life in Art* Stanislavsky explains how he found the image for Kroutitsky in the appearance of an old house, "standing somewhat askew in an older courtyard, and seemingly swollen and overgrown with mossy side beards! From this house ran out little old men in undress uniforms with many unnecessary papers and projects à la General Kroutitsky under their arms." This picture of the crumbling Tsarist empire delighted Lenin when he saw the Moscow Art

Theatre's *Too Clever By Half* shortly after the Revolution in 1918, and he praised the production as agit-prop in the best sense of the term.

In 1923, for the one hundredth anniversary of the playwright's birth, the Soviet Commissar of Education, Anatoly Lunacharsky, who was responsible for cultural policies about the stage, proclaimed a new slogan, "Back to Ostrovsky," which called on revolutionary theatre artists to revise their negative attitude to the classics. In response theatres throughout the Soviet Union embarked on stagings of the nineteenth-century playwright. The most famous and radical of all of these was Sergei Eisenstein's version of *Too Clever By Half*, given at the theatre of the Proletkult (an organization formed after the Revolution to foster art among workers and further agitation and propaganda). Actually what Eisenstein did was not to go back to Ostrovsky, but to bring Ostrovsky into the 1920s. "My aim," he explained, "was to achieve a revolutionary modernization of Ostrovsky, i.e. a social reevaluation of his characters, seeing them as they might appear today."

This period was also a transitional one, characterized by a restructuring of finances designed to restore the economy, which had been devastated by five years of revolution and civil war. In 1921 the New Economic Policy (NEP) had been instituted, allowing a certain amount of free enterprise and giving rise to a breed of bourgeois entrepreneurs known as NEPmen. In this, his first independent work for the theatre, the future film director transformed Ostrovsky's play into a topical social and political satire, ridiculing religion and NEP capitalism, presented in the style of the circus, music hall, and variety show. In his seminal essay, "Montage of Attractions," which he wrote for the production, Eisenstein outlined his theory of scenic composition on which he based drastic reworkings of classic texts—"The spectator himself constitutes the basic material of the theatre."

The rewritten text and scenario of *Too Clever By Half*, with added jokes, puns, and buffoonery, follow the main lines of Ostrovsky's play, but transfer the action to the contemporary Soviet political scene and take us to Paris among the circle of white Russian emigres, permitting added satire on spies and secret agents. The performers functioned as clowns and acrobats, walking over the auditorium on ropes, jumping down in parachutes, and climbing up to the ceiling on poles—without benefit of nets or safety wires. In an epilogue filled with stunts and tricks, Eisenstein used film for the first time in the form of parodies of newsreels and American detective serials with motorized chases. At the end of the performance, as the audience applauded, Eisenstein himself appeared on the screen, smiling and bowing.

Too Clever By Half can take as many guises as Gloumov himself. When in 1965 a guest director from the Leningrad Bolshoi Theatre, Georgii Tovstonogov, staged Ostrovsky's play both in Warsaw and in West Berlin with resident companies (and later at home with his own troupe), he demonstrated that Gloumov is a man of all countries and all seasons. No longer viewed primarily as a comedy of manners determined by its nineteenth-century milieu, Ostrovsky's play speaks directly to contemporary audiences about the problem of honesty in a lying, hypocritical society. Does the bureaucratic system create and cultivate rascals for its own convenience, absolving the individual of his crimes, or is each and every one of us responsible for the existing state of affairs? These are the questions raised by the inwardly truthful Gloumov as he turns on those who have first promoted him and then cast him off and rips through the pretenses of a corrupt older generation. In his final accusatory speeches, according to Tovstonogov, Gloumov is like the magician who discloses the secrets of his art, since at this point he has nothing more to lose, his diary already having revealed his bitter and just condemnation of society.

The ending of *Too Clever By Half* is indeed remarkable, showing, I believe, all the strengths of Ostrovsky's unorthodox dramaturgy. Instead of the moralizing finality and meting out of rewards and punishments usual in comedy, the Russian playwright refuses to "wrap things up," preferring simply to stop in mid-stream. The denouement comes about in the most natural fashion possible—by chance. Aided by the fortune-teller Maniefa, as well as his mother and various servants (all in his pay), Gloumov stages his most impressive show when he makes his prophesied entry into Tourousina's fanatical household. But Mamaev's wife, the amorous Kleopatra—with whom Gloumov has played the passionate lover from a popular romance, scarcely able to control his feelings—learns of his marriage plans and grows jealous; when she accidentally finds the diary carelessly left on Gloumov's desk, the grievously hurt lady turns it over to the disgruntled blackmailer, Golutvin, who uses it to write a scurrilous article in the press and then sends it to the assembled group at Tourousina's.

Here is the point at which Ostrovsky's originality becomes evident. Read aloud, the diary (a major character, not simply a plot device) leads to Gloumov's momentary downfall, but at the same time vindicates him by testifying to his honesty. Addressing in turn his patrons whom he has deceived, the scoundrel at bay forces each to admit that he wished to be deluded and has in no way been harmed or wronged. Once again in possession of his diary, which he can now display publicly as a talisman, Gloumov goes on the offensive, insisting that he is no worse than they are morally, having only acted out their desires, and that he is intellectually much their superior. He will withdraw, but they will regret it.

The exposure of the rogue-hero proves to be his triumph.

At the moment of his defeat, Gloumov turns the tables on his accusers, adopting yet a new role—that of outraged honesty. Before he sought them, now they will seek him. Before he needed them, now they need him. His prediction is immediately fulfilled as the little social circle quickly recognizes that a bright young man like Gloumov is indispensable, and there is an immediate clamor for his return. Who now is "too clever by half"—Gloumov or his eager patrons? The proverbial saying is double-edged.

Gloumov has not only become an enduring character on the Russian stage, but the abstract noun derived from his name, *gloumovshchina* (or Gloumovism), has entered the language. As long as ambitious young men with brains and talent can most readily achieve success by selling themselves and betraying their better natures, Gloumovism will thrive. Transitional societies have a special need of Gloumov to keep things moving—as well as to maintain equilibrium—since the actor-opportunist will further any cause, switch positions overnight, defend opposite sides of the same issue, and turn his coat with every wind until he almost becomes the coat. Since Ostrovsky's aesthetics permit us to speculate about the after-life of his characters, we can imagine that on his return Gloumov will be allowed to keep his diary ("write for the desk drawer"), where he can express his disgust, if only he will serve society and enact its wishes.

SELECTED BIBLIOGRAPHY

Hoover, Marjorie. *Alexander Ostrovsky*. Boston: Twayne, 1981.

Karlinsky, Simon. *Russian Drama from Its Beginnings to the Age of Pushkin*. Berkeley: University of California, 1985.

Mirsky, D.S. *A History of Russian Literature from Its Beginnings to 1900*. Edited by Francis J. Whitfield. New York: Vintage Books, 1958.

Slonim, Marc. *Russian Theater from the Empire to the Soviets*. New York: Collier Books, 1962.

Wettlin, Margaret. "Alexander Ostrovsky and the Russian Theatre before Stanislavsky," in *Alexander Ostrovsky: Plays*, translated by Margaret Wettlin. Moscow: Progress Publishers, 1974.

Made in the USA
Lexington, KY
10 October 2013